FIGHTING The Odds:
From DISAPPROVAL to SELF-ACCEPTANCE

- Domestic Violence
- Molestation
- Date rape
- Depression
- Teen pregnancy
- Low self-esteem

Dr. Kimberlyn Negret

FIGHTING AGAINST THE ODDS:

FROM DISAPPROVAL TO SELF-ACCEPTANCE

Copyright © 2023 Kimberlyn Negret

All publishing rights belong to Kimberlyn Negret.

ISBN: 9798851233654

Printed in the United States of America.

All rights reserved under International Copyright Law.

Contents and/or cover may not be reproduced in whole or in part in any form without the express written consent of the author.

Cover Designs & Illustrations:

Fresh Spirit Publishing Graphics Team

Interior Design: Cassandra Mouton, MHRM, MBA

Chief Editor: Tonya "Toni" Netters

Production Management: Dr. Conte Terrell

To:

_____

From:

_____

Dr. Kimberlyn Negret

TRIBUTE

Learning to live with little regrets has afforded me a peace that surpasses all understanding that could only come from God. The good that has happened has been by the Grace of God. The bad that has happened has taken place with much grace and mercy to endure. I have but one regret, and that is my mother would not live to see my book finished. On July 20, 2012, at 12:05 a.m., my mother, Brenda Ann Millon Gibson, went into eternal rest with our Heavenly Father. Therefore, this book is written as a tribute to her life of tenacity, and stick-to-ittiveness. She was a God-fearing Mother, Grandmother and Great Grandmother anyone would be proud to have.

"For I am already being poured out like a drink offering and the time has come for my departure. I have fought the good fight, I have finished the race, and I have kept the faith. Now, there is in store for me the crown of righteousness, which the Lord, the righteous Judge, will award to me on that day—and

not only to me, but also to all who have longed for His appearing." 2 Timothy 4:6-8

Table of Contents

Introduction.. *13*

Chapter 1: Generations of Strength *15*

Chapter 2: The Longing *17*

Chapter 3: Anointed for Trials *19*

Chapter 4: Broken Promises.................................. *29*

Chapter 5: Shoes, Shoes, Shoes............................. *35*

Chapter 6 : Red Lights, Blue Lights, Sirens!........ *39*

Chapter 7: Careful With Your Words! *45*

Chapter 8: Me and Leah.. *47*

Chapter 8: Leah 2.0.. *53*

Chapter 9: Pressed!!!.. *57*

Chapter 10: It's Always My Fault!!!! *61*

Chapter 11: On the Road Again… *65*

Chapter 12: A Dream Deferred.............................. *67*

Chapter 13: The Second Time Around.................. *81*

Chapter 14: On My Own 85

Chapter 15: A Dream Deferred No Longer 89

Chapter 16: A Tragic Mistake! 93

Chapter 17: The Breaking Begins 103

Chapter 18: Single For The First Time 111

Chapter 19: The Other Face of Ministry! Jezebel Is In the House! 117

Chapter 20: A Prophetic Encounter 131

Chapter 21: More Forgiveness 139

The Aftermath of Hurricane Katrina 139

Chapter 22: Forgiveness 2.0 147

Chapter 23: The Jezebel Spirit: More Learning 157

Chapter 24: Can These Dry Bones Live? 161

Chapter 25: Lifeline 167

Chapter 26: The Deadly Dating Game! 169

About the Author 195

FIGHTING AGAINST THE ODDS:

FROM DISAPPROVAL TO SELF-ACCEPTANCE

Fighting Against the Odds

Dr. Kimberlyn Negret

Introduction

In spite of all the obstacles that have come my way, I now realize that *"the effective prayer of a righteous man can accomplish much."* *(James 5:16)* I thank God for the prayers that were offered up for my family, siblings, my children, and me. I will continue to carry the mantle that has been placed on my life, as it is written:

"The Spirit of the Lord GOD is upon me, Because the LORD has anointed me To bring good news to the afflicted; He has sent me to bind up the brokenhearted, To proclaim liberty to captives And freedom to prisoners; To proclaim the favorable year of the LORD And the day of vengeance of our God; To comfort all who mourn, To grant those who mourn in Zion, Giving them a garland instead of ashes, The oil of gladness instead of mourning, The mantle of praise instead of a spirit of fainting. So they will be called oaks of righteousness, the planting of the LORD, that He may be glorified." Isaiah 61:1-3

I now know my purpose, and I am able to walk in God's alignment while assisting others with discovering their divine purpose and destiny in Christ. I pray that this book empowers, motivates and blesses you.

Chapter 1: Generations of Strength

Trekking through darkness, hostility and shadows of death, Louvenia Hunter set out in search of freedom and a better life. She was my great-great-great-great grandmother and a slave on the Hunter Plantation in Natchez, Mississippi. At the tender age of eleven, she was warned by her brother to flee Mississippi and to follow the river to New Orleans. She was told that the slaves were treated better there, and he wanted that for his sister.

What an unimaginable journey, a monumental task, to travel from Natchez, Mississippi to New Orleans, all alone at that age. She would be leaving her family behind with the realization that she may never see them again. That is exactly what happened. My mind often wonders, What was she thinking as she hid from the slave catchers?" Maneuvering through the brush and threat of the wild, during the nighttime, and evading the slave catchers all while rationing her food and water to make sure she had enough for the trip was daunting at best. As I've journeyed through my own life, I've often pondered many questions regarding her state of resiliency. "How was she to know when she reached her destination?" Listening to her in the spirit, I could hear her conversation with God, asking Him, "God, will You truly provide for me? Are You really a shelter in the time of a storm, food when I'm hungry, and a Mother to the Motherless?"

Since her Mother was too old to leave the plantation, and her brother was captured while attempting to escape, she became an orphan. Tragically, her brother never made it to New Orleans, but was lynched. However, without all the luxuries of maps and GPS, Louvenia made it. She escaped the chains of slavery just as we break the chains of bondage in our lives. Because she made it, I can now make it. The tenacity she embodied helps me to keep going, even when I feel that my journey has me traveling through the brush, at night, with chains binding me. With her blood flowing through my veins, I know I will make it. Now, with two generations looking to me to make it. I must!

Chapter 2: The Longing

My journey is not of a geographical, but a spiritual nature. Pursuing intimacy with God is my life's mission. This journey is one that has taken me through the *"thickets of life and breaking of chains"*, across spiritual peaks and valleys and, in some cases, the wilderness. Ultimately, my prayer has been that my journey will end when I meet with my Master and hear those faithful words, *"Well done, good and faithful servant! You have been faithful with a few things; I will put you in charge of many things. Come and share in your master's happiness!" Matthew 25:23*

Born in New Orleans, Louisiana and raised in the Catholic Church, I followed the Catholic faith from the time I was a small child until about the age of nineteen. Although I had gone through the ritual ceremony of my First Communion, I never completed my Confirmation, nor was I confirmed. When I was nineteen years old, I joined a small Baptist church and began to feel what I know now as the Holy Spirit. After attending that church for many years, I began to thirst for more again. So, my search for God continued and after several years, I eventually left that church and joined a more contemporary church. My void was deafening and seeking the authenticity of God was my lifeline. I longed to know Him on a deeper and more personal level. I realized that each church was a steppingstone and a piece of my spiritual puzzle. Therefore, I learned that no one church had it all, which is why I needed a relationship with God that transcends the physical church. Once I understood that equation, I sought and craved my quiet time with God which always filled me to overflowing and diminished my disappointment with church people.

"As the deer pants for the water brooks, so my soul pants for you, O God. My soul thirsts for God, for the living God; when shall I come and appear before God?" Psalm 42:1-2

Chapter 3: Anointed for Trials

December 27th, May 31st, and March 30th marked significant events dear to my heart. Those are the dates that my grandbabies were born. I was blessed to have been there for their births and to anoint them with oil as they left their mother's womb. There were also graduations, ordinations, and promotions; all good things and life events that I am so very proud of. As a Mother and Grandmother, I consider it an honor to be their priest, provider, and protector, just like God has been for me. But that nostalgia had not always been present.

I was about seven years old when "it" happened. It was a Saturday morning. I remember hearing my grandmother shuffling to go to the grocery store. We stayed over at her house because my mom had to work the overnight shift. I'm not quite sure where my Father was. As she scurried around, I remember lying in the bed, hoping against hope that she wouldn't leave. I knew, somehow, that if she left "it" would happen.

You see, my grandfather was a child molester. He used to sit me on his lap and fondle himself. For some reason, I knew that today would be worse than others. I and two of my other siblings used to sleep on a queen-sized mattress on the floor of my grandmother's room when we stayed over. This was before the days of air mattresses. For whatever reason, Maw-Maw and Paw-Paw didn't sleep in the same room. He usually slept on the sofa-sleeper in the living room.

This particular day, Maw-Maw left the house to go to the store. What I remember most was laying there, waiting, fearing that the "boogie man" was going to come and get me. He did. I remember lying very still, as if I were asleep, almost corpse-like. It did not faze him. He carried me out of the room into the living room where the sofa-sleeper laid open. He placed me on the bed, pulled my underwear down, placed his privates between my legs, and began to molest me. This was the first time that he had actually gotten me alone. From that point on, I would never be the same. For whatever reason, he stopped, and I continued to lay there like a zombie.

These incidents started a downward spiral in my life. What I learned, first and foremost, was that I was not safe, not even at my grandparent's home. My innocence had no value because my grandfather had taken it away from me. Those that should have protected me, didn't.

Reflecting on this traumatic experience at such a young age, reminds me of the story in the Bible of Amnon's violation of his own sister, Tamar. He abused his position of trust, not only with her, but with everyone he made a pawn in his diabolical plot to seduce her and steal her virtue. (*2 Samuel 13: 1-20*) So as that happened to Tamar, it happened to me.

To add insult to injury, he used to call me his "birthday girl". Yes, that's right; I was born on his birthday. Everyone was under the impression that I was special because of that, when indeed it was that he had been violating me. No one knew the dark scary secret that I carried into my adulthood. What an ungodly soul-tie to have. Yet, it was my burden to carry until it wasn't. Like a ragdoll draped around my neck, hanging down my back, it was with me everywhere I went. I didn't know how I would ever escape its grasp, so I made due as best as I could.

After moving back home from Texas to finish college, my grandfather came over to our house. He knocked on the door and I looked out of the window and saw that it was him. Home alone and paralyzed with fear, I felt as though I was seven-years-old all over again. Although I was safe inside, behind locked doors, with bars on the windows, I was terrified thinking that my safety would be jeopardized again. Even though I was a grown woman now, I still felt so vulnerable. At times, my fear may have seemed irrational, but to me it was a reality. Yes, it had been years since I was violated, but the scars were still fresh. I realized that they stayed fresh because I never tended to them. Much like a wound that was never treated, it attempted to take its natural course of healing and simply adapted to function and survive. However, this time, I was strong enough and old enough to take control. Like a predator stalking his prey, he sat. Determined not to be caught and devoured, I sat. Today was the day I would maintain my safety, my dignity, and my peace. The Lord made my mountain stand strong and I refused to open the door. As I continued to peer out of the window, he prowled the perimeter of the home. He had some nerve! Knowing that my car was outside and that he was stubborn enough to sit a while, I waited him out. At that point in my life, I had already erased my sentimental grandfather image and took him at face value.

Eventually, he left, and I wiped the sweat off my forehead. I thanked God for strengthening and protecting me. Later on, he had the audacity to tell my mother that I wouldn't let him take advantage of the façade he's been perpetrating since I was a child. Because my mother didn't know of the abuse, I told her that one of my friends came by and picked me up. What a tormenting mind game victims/survivors are manipulated to play! Who was I trying to protect and why was it necessary? At that time, it seemed as though I was protecting everybody's feelings but my own. Ironically, I remember my mother stating that if anyone ever touched us in "that way", she would kill them. I carried that "dirty little secret" around because I didn't want my mother or my father in jail and, more importantly, I was not prepared to deal with all that would come with telling the truth about my grandfather.

For a while, I was really angry with my mother. I know you're probably asking, "Why would she be angry with her mother for the acts of her father?" My answer is that my parents and grandmother knew my grandfather had the propensity to perpetrate. You see, many years later, I learned that he had molested my mother the same way that he molested me. Totally insane, right? Logically speaking, if you know someone has a vile tendency toward children or anyone else for that matter, why would you allow that person to have access to them? That's a question I pondered perpetually for a long time. And frankly, I could not wrap my head around it at all.

As a survivor, addressing this lack of reporting abuse of any kind in the African American community is critical. As a people, we must work to eradicate this "curse" if we want to truly protect our children. The scars of abuse are far-reaching and can no longer be ignored. Just as Absalom stepped in and avenged his disgraced, injured, abused, defenseless sister, someone must step in and offer help. That someone just might be you, *"For such a time as this." Esther 4:14*

For years, I thought, "Why did you put your children in harm's way? Why did you let us visit him? You knew that he was a predator!" I would learn later that the only One that could release me from all my anger would be God *(2 Samuel 13: 1-19)*. However, this would happen much later. It would take years of emotional, mental, and spiritual processing before healing, deliverance, and restoration could take place.

Sidebar

Child sexual abuse is a significant public health problem and an *Adverse Childhood Experience* *(ACE)*. Child sexual abuse refers to the involvement of a child (person less than 18 years old) in sexual activity that violates the laws or social taboos of society and that he/she:

- does not fully comprehend

- does not consent to or is unable to give informed consent to, or
- is not developmentally prepared for and cannot give consent to

Many children wait to report or never report child sexual abuse. Therefore, the numbers below likely underestimate the true impact of the problem. Although estimates vary across studies, the research shows:

- About 1 in 4 girls and 1 in 13 boys in the United States experience child sexual abuse.
- Someone known and trusted by the child or child's family members, perpetrates 91% of child sexual abuse.
- The total lifetime economic burden of child sexual abuse in the United States in 2015 was estimated to be at least $9.3 billion. Today, it has at least quadrupled.

Experiencing child sexual abuse can affect how a person thinks, acts, and feels over a lifetime. This can result in short and long-term physical, mental, and behavioral health consequences.

Examples of physical health consequences include:

- sexually transmitted infections (STIs)
- physical injuries
- chronic conditions later in life, such as heart disease, obesity, and cancer

Examples of mental health consequences include:

- depression
- posttraumatic stress disorder (PTSD) symptoms

Examples of behavioral consequences include:

- substance use/misuse, including opioid misuse
- risky sexual behaviors, meaning sex with multiple partners or behaviors that could result in pregnancy or STIs
- increased risk for perpetration of sexual violence
- increased risk for suicide or suicide attempts

Experiencing child sexual abuse can also increase a person's risk for future victimization. For example, recent studies have found:

- Females exposed to child sexual abuse are at 2-13 times increased risk of sexual violence victimization in adulthood
- People who experienced child sexual abuse are at twice the risk for non-sexual intimate partner violence

https://www.cdc.gov/violenceprevention/childsexualabuse/fastfact.html

Chapter 4: Broken Promises

"My people are destroyed for lack of knowledge. Because you have rejected knowledge, I also will reject you from being My priest. Since you have forgotten the law of your God, I also will forget your children." Hosea 4:6

"In the same way, you wives, be submissive to your own husbands so that even if any of them are disobedient to the Word, they may be won without a word by the behavior of their wives, as they observe your chaste and respectful behavior. Your adornment must not be merely external--braiding the hair, and wearing gold jewelry, or putting on dresses; but let it be the hidden person of the heart, with the imperishable quality of a gentle and quiet spirit, which is precious in the sight of God." I Peter 3:1-4

"A gentle answer turns away wrath, but a harsh word stirs up anger." Proverbs 15:1

All I ever really wanted was to be the apple of his eye, my father's eye. As the third of four children, I would fly under the radar unnoticed most of the time. My oldest sister was the "smart one", my brother was the only boy, and my youngest sister was the baby of the family. I remember walking through the house on many occasions wanting my father to play with me; wanting him to talk to me or even acknowledge my existence. There is something about a little girl knowing that her father is exclusively there for her and accepts her just as she is. Being able to climb on his lap, walk in the park with him or just plainly feel safe means the world to her. Unfortunately, that was not the case for me. I remember "it" so clearly.

We lived at 2636 North Johnson Street, and it was Labor Day. I sat on the porch watching all my friends leaving with their parents to go to various destinations, such as Lake Pontchartrain or City Park. I sat on the porch for what seemed like an eternity, waiting for my Dad to show up to take us to the park, or quite honestly, anywhere. He promised he would.

He didn't take us places often, so when he announced that we were going somewhere with him, I desperately wanted to believe in him. Well, minutes turned into hours. My friends returned home, and I came to the reality that my father wasn't coming home to take us anywhere.

Then there was Mardi Gras, one of the biggest free parties in the city of New Orleans. Everyone knows that when you lived in New Orleans, Mardi Gras was the holiday of all holidays. You get a few days off from school and your parents treat you to all sorts of junk food. My favorites were the big red candied apples. I loved catching those legendary beads as you screamed, "Hey Mister, throw me something!" It was always wonderful being a kid during Mardi Gras. This year, it wouldn't happen for us. We were all dressed up with no place to go. Mom figured out where my father was, so she went to "Rick's", his favorite watering spot, to get him. It was for naught because we never made it to the parade. How could I compete with his friends, his alcohol, and the life that went along with it? It was hard enough competing with my siblings, and now I had to compete with my father's all-consuming and contrary lifestyle.

As a little girl, the void of not having his attention was devastating to me. I felt totally invisible. Much later in life, I would learn that there wasn't really a true competition at all, because being a Father never registered with him even though we were his children. In all honesty and fairness, how could I expect my father to be a father to me when actuality he did not have a father to model himself after? Although his mother remarried later on in his life, the damage had already been done. He could only give me what he had and that wasn't much. He never developed the emotional capacity to care for my mom or any of us children. He was raised in the home of his grandparents with several other extended family members but that bonding did not occur. I thank God that he had that family unit, but Father simply couldn't give me what he didn't have or comprehend.

How do you parent and nurture a child when you are broken and empty yourself? I know, understand and feel his pain, but nevertheless, I am released from carrying it. Turning my attention toward the loving parent I did have, I learned how to be a great Mother from my mom. For a long time, I failed to recognize how hard she worked to take care of us in my Father's absence. She would have breakfast ready for us, walk us to school, have dinner ready by the time we got out of school, and then help us with our homework before leaving for her graveyard shift at Charity Hospital. She was a phenomenal woman and Mother.

On the other hand, learning how to be a wife was a different issue. Because my grandfather was abusive toward my mother and grandmother, my mother vowed that a man, not even her husband, would ever control her. My mother didn't really know how to submit. Her harsh environment rendered her incapable of trusting any man enough to submit. When you are not raised under the Word or the admonition of the Lord, you tend to make a lot of mistakes, repeat them, and somehow think that you are right. I carried what I thought was "strength" from my mother into my marriage. Boy was I wrong! I didn't know how to be a wife either. Because I never saw it modeled, submission was foreign to me. On another note, the duality of the situation is that I can't imagine what our lives would have been like if my mother tried to submit to my father who was not in position nor strong enough to be her covering. We would have been homeless I'm sure.

Chapter 5: Shoes, Shoes, Shoes

"Then he reached out his hand and took the knife to slay his son.

"But the Angel of the Lord called out to him from heaven, "Abraham! Abraham!"

"Here I am," he replied.

"Do not lay a hand on the boy," He said. "Do not do anything to him. Now I know that you fear God, because you have not withheld from Me your son, your only son."

Abraham looked up and there in a thicket he saw a ram caught by its horns. He went over and took the ram and sacrificed it as a burnt offering instead of his son.

So, Abraham called that place "The Lord Will Provide." And to this day it is said, "On the mountain of The Lord it will be provided." Genesis 22:10-14

Well, my mother and father finally divorced after twenty years of separating, fussing, fighting and all manner of other chaos. Initially, I was happy because I didn't have to worry about my father coming into the house creating a ruckus anymore. I no longer had to be afraid that he could come in and destroy the house, pull out a gun, or put my mom in a frenzy. I must be honest; he wasn't always the initiator of such disturbances.

Forgiving my father's behavior, indiscretions and absenteeism was hard to reconcile or get over in and of itself. Moreover, it was especially difficult because she had suffered abuse by the hands of her own "father." Considering the circumstances, my mother was intent on letting my father know that although she might not win the fight, he was going to know she was not a push over. So, her harbored animosity towards him sometimes displayed itself without provocation. This changed dramatically after they divorced. They were better off friends than spouses.

What I noticed the most after my parent's divorce was the long hours Mom had to work, merely trying to meet the bills. I remember that although we sometimes ate luncheon meat for breakfast with eggs and toast, luncheon meat sandwiches for lunch, and luncheon meat with mashed potatoes and corn for dinner, we never went hungry. We were never without lights, gas, or water. I remember one school year when Mom worked extra hard to buy us the school clothes we really wanted. Well, it didn't take long for the neighborhood kids to see the fruit of my mother's hard work.

You see, our laundry room was detached from the house, and at this time, our dryer was broken, so we hung our clothes out to dry. We came home one day only to find that our clothes had been stolen off the clothesline. This was just two months into the school year, and it was about to turn cold.

As a result, I remember wearing shorts in late October and pretending that I wasn't cold because I knew that my mother had done all she could to take care of us. This, too, was a source of resentment that I developed toward my father. As my mother worked sixteen-hour shifts to "make do," he drove his Lincoln Continental, wore his tailor-made suits, and lived the glamorous life. Today it's fashionable to purchase clothing with holes in them, but I refuse to do so. I had to wear that before it was fashionable, back in the early 1980s. Then, I remember saving up to purchase a pair of black "ballerina" shoes. I purchased them from Baker's, a shoe store on Canal Street. After wearing them day in and day out for several months, the sole came apart. I remember getting off the Galvez bus and walking about six to eight blocks to my home on Franklin Avenue, dragging my foot the entire way. I didn't want anyone to see that my sole had separated from the shoe. So, I got some crazy glue and glued my shoe back together. I didn't bother to tell my mother; she was already doing all that she could to keep the house running. Now, when I go into my closet, I thank God for the numerous pairs of shoes that I have and a closet of my own. I'm grateful to God for allowing me to recognize how hard my mother worked, and most importantly, I thank Him for being *Jehovah Jireh - "Yahweh will provide."* (*Genesis 22:14*) *Jehovah Jireh* is the name Abraham gave to the place where The Lord provided a sacrifice in place of Isaac. Being that He is the same yesterday, today and forever, He provided for me just the same.

Chapter 6 : Red Lights, Blue Lights, Sirens!

"God is our refuge and strength, a very present help in trouble." Psalm 46:1

Recalling a particularly bad day before my parent's divorce, Mom and Father got into "it" again. Not quite sure what "it" was about, but what I do remember is him hitting her. At the time, my little sister was too young to help, so along with my oldest sister and brother, we got on my Father's back to stop him from hitting my Mom. Doing so allowed her time to run outside to call the police.

"Okay, tell me what happened" the officer asked, speaking to each of us individually. He looked as though he were thirty feet tall. I thought to myself, am I going to lie, or should I tell the truth? If I tell the truth, my father would go off to jail, but if I lied, my mother remains in jeopardy. What a predicament to be in as an eight or nine-year-old child. I thought to myself, "I just don't understand why they can't get along."

After speaking with us, as well as my parents, they decided to leave my Father there. I didn't necessarily want him to go off to jail, but I certainly didn't want him to stay there with us! This was the beginning of my fear of him. A pattern was starting.

Another time we were just watching television and then we heard "it." "It" was a loud crashing sound from the kitchen. My mom was cutting onions with a serrated blade knife. The knife was at least twelve inches long. We ran to the back of the house and my brother stated, "He better not be hitting my momma!" That statement enraged my father, who subsequently approached my brother. He punched my brother across the room. All I could hear was chaos in the back of the house and for a while, I was too scared to move. Although I didn't know anything about the Holy Spirit then, I know now that it was only the Holy Spirit that restrained my mother that day. You see, my father was upset with my mom and took an axe to the refrigerator.

It seemed like an eternity, but we then took off to the kitchen to check on my mother. The next thing we knew was that my mom was "Ms. Celie", from "The Color Purple." In the movie, Ms. Celie and Shug had a strange relationship. Ms. Celie was forced to marry "Mister" and he treated her as though he hated her. Shug Avery was once his lover. Over the course of years, Ms. Celie and Shug Avery formed a deep friendship. Mister was cruel toward Ms. Celie and caused her sister to flee his home after she refused his sexual advances. Ms. Celie and her sister, Nettie, had vowed never to part. With the help of Shug Avery, Ms. Celie found letters written to her by her sister Nettie stating that, "Mister", had been hiding over the years. Ms. Celie was in the field reading some of the letters, where Mister found her. He had gone looking for her because she hadn't heard his "call" to come and shave him, and he slapped her across the face. This shave would be different today. If Shug Avery hadn't asked the children where Ms. Celie was and ran in fear of what she might do, Mister would have been killed that day. Shug Avery arrived at the home in the nick of time to save Mister. So we were "Shug", just as "Ms. Celie" prepared to shave "Mister", her intent being to slice his throat from ear to ear. Something inside of "Shug" had her run to check on "Ms. Celie" and she caught her in time, just before she was going to kill "Mister."

Well on that day, the Holy Spirit arrested my mom, as she had that twelve-inch serrated knife placed against his chest. Her exact words were, "If you ever hit one of my children like that again, I'll drive this knife through your chest!", and she meant it. If my Mom killed my father, she would go off to jail and who would take care of us? The thought of having to live with my sexual abuser was too much to handle. That is when I started praying, "God, please protect us." Those prayers then changed to, "God, please don't let him come home tonight."

After numerous incidents of fights, pulling knives and guns, he simply stopped coming home. It was a lot for a little girl to handle. My, my, I'm not safe at home or at my grandmother's house. I felt as though I was running out of safe havens.

"God is our protection and our strength. He always helps in times of trouble." Psalm 46:1

Fighting Against the Odds

Chapter 7: Careful With Your Words!

"Consider it all joy, my brethren, when you encounter various trials." James 1:2

Although my childhood was tumultuous, my parents did teach us some good lessons. I remember my father telling us to, "Work smart, not hard." He would always encourage - okay preach - to us that we should get our education because that would be our way out.

One Friday afternoon, my father saw me getting off the bus without any books. He told me that he didn't care if the other kids didn't bring books home over the weekend, but WE were going to! If we didn't have homework, believe me, he would make some up.

Vividly recalling my ninth-grade graduation, I remember my father asking if I was going to be one of the top ten students in my grade. I told him, "No", but I was in the top ten percent of the class. His remark was, "I could've stayed home." This statement was a crushing blow to me. Once again, I didn't cut the mustard. My oldest sister graduated from high school the same month and ranked number three in the top ten and had received numerous scholarship offers and awards. Was I ever going to match up to any of my siblings? I would spend years trying to win the approval of my father. Ironically, the thought occurred how he's never met one of my expectations, but has the nerve to place demands on me. How peculiar is that? My mom also encouraged us to become whatever we wanted. When it came to school, there were no excuses. Just get it done.

Chapter 8: Me and Leah

Seeds of poor self-esteem, and promiscuity coupled with feelings of hopelessness and despair, finally bloomed as I reached puberty. Because I didn't genuinely know how to accept love from a male, and to be honest, it was a long time before I would learn, my life started to take a turn for the worst.

"So, Leah became pregnant with Reuben for she said, "Because The Lord has seen my affliction, surely now my husband will love me." Then there was Simeon, "For the Lord has heard that I am unloved." Then there was Levi, "Surely my husband would become attached to me." Then there was Judah, "This time I will praise the Lord" and she stopped bearing children." Genesis 29:32 – 35

Leah, Leah. Imagine your father having to trick someone into marrying you. What a great esteem booster! As if that were not enough, once the marriage was consummated, your husband turns around and decided that he would go back to the drawing board to work for the woman he wanted initially, your sister. Therefore, in her quest for "love" she bore child after child after child, hopelessly thinking that her husband would love her. I was Leah. I began seeking intimacy to feel loved, only to find out that what I was seeking, I could only find in Christ.

At age sixteen, I became pregnant with my daughter. The reproach I had always felt since being molested finally manifested outwardly. My mother was devastated by the news and my father's statements cut like a knife. I remember him asking my mother, "What kind of whorehouse are you running around here?" He had spoken correctly. My mother was running the house, alone! He was living elsewhere in New Orleans but checked in from time to time.

After his statement, I thought, "Man, what a way to be thought of by your own father, the man that you desired to love you and to be proud of you, but never did." I would spend a lifetime trying to "right that wrong." Trying to mitigate the shame I thought I had brought upon the family, I spent years trying to seek his approval. Even more upsetting was the fact that I continued a generational curse. This would be the fourth generation of children born out of wedlock. Since 1924, in my family, every twenty years saw the birth of a female child, out of wedlock. This was most definitely a curse!

My first child was brought into this world because I needed to feel loved. I wish that I could say that I truly loved the Father of my child, but how could I have loved him when I didn't know how to love? I only dated him because I was at one of the lowest points of my life. Recently broken up with the "love of my life", I found out that he had been dating someone else, a preacher's daughter. He was a church musician, raised in the church, and I was "just a heathen." How could I possibly compete with that? Again, I was no match. He was the first person that I ever talked to about the molestation. It didn't help that my father ran him away from the house in one of his tirades. I guess he thought that my baggage was far too much to deal with. How could I really expect an eighteen-year-old teenager to be able to handle all my issues? So, we broke up and I was devastated.

Several months later, I woke up excited about my sixteenth birthday. Isn't this supposed to be one of the greatest days of a young girl's life? Well, as the day progressed, nothing… absolutely nothing, happened. I kept thinking that surely something would happen, but by day's end, not even a cake appeared. "How could my mother forget my birthday?", I wondered. Well, Mom didn't forget, she just didn't have the money to buy anything, let alone a cake. It wasn't that she didn't want to, it was that she couldn't. As a Mother now, I am certain that it truly was as hurtful for her as it was for me.

Later, I got a call and was invited to celebrate my birthday at Jaeger's, a pretty cool restaurant in New Orleans, so I went. Additionally, I got a bottle of cologne, "Chanel No.3." Not long after that date, I gave up my prized possession for those trinkets. I traded the irreplaceable for something with little to no value.

Dr. Kimberlyn Negret

Here it is, February 1984, and I was pregnant with my daughter. Needless to say, after trying to keep a relationship built on this shaky foundation, and being only sixteen years old, the relationship crumbled. I grew up and aspired of college and a better life for my daughter, but my daughter's father didn't see the need. Although college was an expectation, I secretly wanted to drop out. Hesitant to return to school, I just knew that the stigma of having a baby out of wedlock would be present on me like the Scarlet Letter. However, there was also an expectation that my parents had, and that was for their children to obtain a college degree. Because my daughter's father and I had different upbringings, values and belief systems, our roads came to an impasse, and we parted ways.

Fighting Against the Odds

Chapter 8: Leah 2.0

In 1987, I began dating my now ex-husband. There were enough red flags that a blind person would have seen them and had the sense to run, but not me. I thought to myself, "he's not that bad, and this is probably as good as it's going to get for me, so I might as well take the plunge." In 1989, we married, and soon afterward, we moved to Illinois, as that was where he was stationed in the Navy. I was now married to something I feared. Although he was always a good provider, a "protector and priest" he was not. I spent countless years, about fourteen, walking on eggshells to keep him from fussing, making excuses for his selfishness and enduring his cruel intentions. His excessive beatings on my kids, and the emotional and verbal abuse I suffered was a nightmare. For most of the courtship and marriage, I was ridiculed about my weight. Years later, we would find out that I had a medical condition, polycystic ovarian syndrome, that caused my unexplained weight gain and acne. Ultimately, I had a hysterectomy in 2007.

Gentlemen would comment on how nice I looked, but all that I would hear resonating in my mind was, "You can't possibly think you look good in that, do you"? Unfortunately, that was the only opinion that counted to me. Then I came to the realization, *"For thus says the Lord of Hosts: He sent me after glory, to the nations which plunder you; for he who touches you touches the apple of His eye." (Zechariah 2:8)* I didn't yet know that I was the apple of God's eye.

In December 1989, after seven short months of marriage, my heart was crushed. My ex-husband was stationed in Great Lakes, Illinois, and I had only been in the state for two months. As I was cleaning the refrigerator one day, he blurted, "That is what I liked about my ex-girlfriend. She had "get up and go about herself." He was referring to the fact that I had not yet found a job. It was difficult because I was new in town, needed to secure daycare for my child, and I didn't drive. I remember thinking to myself, "And I married him because..?" He has taken me away from home, over twelve hundred miles from my family. I don't know anyone, and you compare me with the woman you cheated on me with? I guess the honeymoon was over.

August of 1990, I gave birth to our son. Then in November 1990, I moved back to New Orleans. He was then stationed in San Diego. I thought that it would be a great time to finish my degree. Later, I found out that the only reason he agreed to my returning home was because he thought that I would fall apart, be unsuccessful and end up in San Diego, with him. *"But as for you, you meant evil against me; but God meant it for good, in order to bring it about as it is this day, to save many people alive."* Genesis 50:20

Well, it didn't happen that way. For the first time in my life, I had a checking account, learned how to drive, and cared for my two children as I matriculated. The kids and I lived with my mother, and I was able to get us out of thousands of dollars of credit card debt in three years, off of military pay. No easy feat! My journey had taken me from New Orleans to Texas, to Illinois and back again to New Orleans. I then vowed he would never take me away from my home again. Wrong!

"For this reason a man shall leave his father and his mother and be joined to his wife; and they shall become one flesh." *(Genesis 2:24)* I guess I didn't quite have the aforementioned scripture right, yet.

Chapter 9: Pressed!!!

"We are hard pressed on every side, but not crushed; perplexed, but not in despair; 9 persecuted, but not abandoned; struck down, but not destroyed." 2 Corinthians 4: 8-9

In May 1992, I was pressed in another way. My mother, whom I held dear to me, became ill in church. By this time, I had been baptized and attended church regularly. We left the church and, with much resistance from her, took my mother to the emergency room. Once there, we were told that she had suffered a massive heart attack and that we should get our family members to New Orleans as soon as possible. I remember having this feeling of hopelessness as I slid down the wall of the waiting room. That night, I held the Bible real close to my heart and I told God, I don't know where to find it in this book, but I needed Him to heal my mother. I didn't know where to find the scripture, but I had faith.

"Now faith is the assurance of things hoped for, the conviction of things not seen." Hebrews 11:1

Approximately two weeks later, my mother was home and boy, were we happy! My family usually worshiped together at our local church. However, after this life-changing event, I knew that I needed to find a church that would feed my newfound hunger for the Word. Shortly thereafter, I would leave our family church in a quest for a "Word" church - and I would find it. It was really difficult to leave the church where my family worshipped. However, the timing was right. Needless to say, once the enemy finds out that you are on a quest to have a closer relationship with Christ, he unleashes all of his demons. My daughter would start to act out in school and slipped out of the house one night to go to a party. I would soon learn to fast and pray!

"But this kind does not go out except by prayer and fasting." Matthew 17:21

Dr. Kimberlyn Negret

In May 1993, my ex-husband arrived home from the military, but I was not happy to see him. Months prior to him coming home, we had not been getting along. Imagine that. We were living over one thousand miles apart and we could not get along. Prior to him coming home, I told him that I wanted a divorce, but he didn't listen. He came home and things were hostile. I really didn't want him there. I guess I was just tired. Eventually, I gave in, and we began to work on our marriage, or so I thought. We purchased a home and began living the "American Dream". I had already finished my bachelor's degree and he started pursuing his again. Unfortunately, he would never earn his. We'll talk about this more in the next segment.

Fighting Against the Odds

Chapter 10: It's Always My Fault!!!!

"Therefore, there is now no condemnation for those who are in Christ Jesus." Romans 8:1

It was all my fault:

1. When the children acted out.
2. That I was overweight, and he wasn't happy in the marriage.
3. That he didn't finish college.
4. There wasn't enough meat in the beans.

Yes, I took the blame for it all. It was my fault when the children acted out because I wasn't strict enough. In his absence, and while he was away in the Navy, I learned to care for the kids as best as I knew how and still, that wasn't enough. He thought that I was too lenient with the kids and my punishments weren't swift or harsh enough.

It was my fault that I was overweight. I guess he thought that I just ate too much, giving no credence to my

PCOS. This condition would cause multiple cysts to form on my ovaries, along with massive weight gain, hair loss, and severe pustule acne. Now, if all of that wasn't enough, I had to deal with him being more concerned about my weight than my actual health. I remember telling him that I had found out what was wrong with me and he stated he just wanted me to lose the weight.

I was so frustrated. On a quest for years, trying to find out what was wrong with me, I went from doctor to doctor, only to end up diagnosing myself through careful research and then having the doctor confirm the diagnosis. My ex-husband was a body builder; so much of his extra time was spent lifting weights. With his propensity to work out, he wasn't empathetic toward me at all. Trying to appeal to some sensitivity, if there was any, I often told him that I would still care for him if he became ill or even God forbid, lose a limb. Either it went right over his head or his heart wasn't having it. I just don't think he got it. It was my fault that he wasn't happy in the marriage. Nothing was ever good enough. The house was never clean enough, there wasn't enough meat in the beans, blah, blah, blah....

It was my fault that he didn't finish college. One lesson my parents taught me was that we needed to take our schoolwork seriously. I don't think that was a popular stance with my husband. Although my ex-husband worked hard in college after his release from the military, he wouldn't finish the courses he needed to complete his degree program. I remember him once asking me to do a paper for him. I told him that I would be more than happy to assist him, however, I could not, in good conscience, complete the paper for him. He rationalized that since I was good at it, I should just do it. For a while, I thought that he was joking, until I saw by his countenance that he was serious. Not only that, but he was mad! I did not relent. I had to do the right thing. I needed to be able to live with myself.

During Christmas in 1997, my mother-in-law and father-in-law came to visit. I must admit, I was not the best company. My ex and I were not getting along again. I had made up in my mind that I was going to speak with his father for some insight. I was desperate. If I didn't get some help soon, I was going to lose it. After several hours of speaking with my in-laws, my father-in-law told my mother-in-law, "I don't understand my son; all she is asking for is to feel loved and appreciated." I guess that was a daunting task for him. As time went on, our relationship continued to sour. It was at this time that we first attempted marriage counseling. I said 'attempted' because after the first two sessions, he didn't like that the therapist said, "Maybe you should separate." He stated that he didn't agree with that, and he certainly wasn't going to pay for that kind of advice. In retrospect, I agreed with his assessment of the situation. If we were going to seek counseling about our marriage, we needed to seek Christian Counseling.

Chapter 11: On the Road Again…

One morning, we got a call from Grandma, my mother-in-law, telling us that my father-in-law had a heart attack and that the paramedics were there performing CPR. She stated we better get there quickly. As we loaded the car, she called back and stated that he passed away. How was I supposed to tell my husband that his father passed and we still had to make a 6 ½ hour drive to Houston? I carried that burden for the entire ride. I remember listening to Fred Hammond's "No Weapon" over and over and over during the trip and it got me through. We arrived in Houston and my mother-in-law told him that his father was gone.

His father came to the United States from Cuba at the age of seventeen to play baseball. He did not know the English language and had very little finances. However, he did come with a valuable trade, upholstery. His baseball dream did not work out so, he began working in upholstery. Eventually, he opened his own upholstery shop, which my ex-husband took over after his father's death. This was the reason that I relocated to Houston with him. Even though I contemplated divorce during the 1997 Christmas season, after his father passed, I realized that was certainly not the time to leave my now-ex-husband.

It was August 1998 and I remember the incident quite clearly. As I fixed breakfast, my husband asked me to do a favor for him. I replied, "Sure, what is it?" His reply was, "Would you lose weight for me?" I thought to myself, "Here we go again. This is the second time you got me away from my family and you start this nagging mess. Your father just died two months ago, we're trying to sell our home in Gretna (Louisiana), run a business here, register the kids in school, and all you can think of is me losing weight? Good grief!"

Chapter 12: A Dream Deferred

Then the Lord answered me and said, "Record the vision and inscribe it on tablets, that the one who reads it may run. For the vision is yet for the appointed time; it hastens toward the goal and it will not fail, though it tarries, wait for it; for it will certainly come, it will not delay." Habakkuk 2:2-3

By the time we left Louisiana, I had just been accepted into the Criminal Justice graduate program at Southern University at New Orleans. I was devastated that I would not be able to attend, but family came first. In the fall of 1999, I applied for admission to Our Lady of the Lake University graduate program in Houston and remembered getting ready for the interview. My older sister was visiting Houston and she told me, "Go and get it!". She believed in me when I did not believe in myself. I got accepted into the program! To God be the glory!

Taking on this challenge would prove to be one of the most stressful times of my life. This is the point where I started to embody the *"Proverbs 31 woman."* Sleep? What was that? Who needed it? I was working full time at a transitional housing program for homeless youth, working with my ex-husband in the upholstery business, helping to deliver furniture, bookkeeping, and invoicing. I was still tasked with cooking, caring for the kids, and being a wife. Oh, I forgot to mention that I was also in graduate school.

Well, the spring of 2000 would find me in a women's shelter. While in graduate school, I was in a study group with someone who worked at a local women's shelter. I told her about my situation at home. On this particular Sunday, we had just left church, drove over to Kroger to get some groceries, and "it" happened. It was like my ex-husband was the "hulk". He would go from zero to sixty in a second. He became upset with our daughter and went off on her in the store. She was about thirteen or fourteen, and I could feel her embarrassment. He was upset about her not praising and worshipping like he wanted her to at church. The pastor had spoken with all the youth regarding their level of praise. She had not been singled out so there was no need to berate her like that. As my ex-husband began to reprimand her, I left her there. I thought that if I were there, it would just get worse so, I walked off. I went to the car and called my brother-in-law to tell him what was going on. Needless to say, we didn't finish our grocery shopping and that situation was the last straw, at least for now.

My ex-husband worked from 6:00 PM in the evening to 6:00 AM in the morning. Now was the time to "bust a move". I took the kids to my mother-in-law's home and waited until he went to work. When the coast was clear, I went back home and called the shelter. After following their protocol, I was told to go to a specific pay phone for further instructions. At about 2:00 AM in the morning, we were allowed admittance into the shelter.

The shelter experience is something that neither I nor my kids will ever forget. I remember it so clearly. My children were huddled in a twin bed with me as it was set up like a college dormitory room. It had four bunk beds and two dressers in one room. Somehow, I knew that I would not be staying there long. Not that the shelter was inappropriate, it was just very different from home, and quite honestly, we were having a very rough time adjusting. I don't know if it was the closed-circuit televisions, the alarm systems, or just the fear in the other women's eyes, but it was an awakening. We got settled in and were told when to arrive for breakfast. I was concerned about how I would get my kids to school. Then the thought occurred, "Wait a minute! If I took them to school "it" could happen. He could go to the school and get them." As my mind continued processing all the "what ifs", I assimilated to the shelter's morning routine. The kids and I proceeded downstairs for breakfast and when we got downstairs, I was given an assignment, a chore to help wash the massive amounts of dishes. They must have had the largest pots in the ENTIRE world. Anyway, the kids only wanted cereal, so as I went to prepare their cereal, my daughter just burst in tears. She was not accustomed to this type of lifestyle. Although our home life was pretty scary, we were not familiar with the "faces of abuse" of this magnitude. We roomed with a woman that had just been released from the hospital, with broken ribs, a broken nose, and black eyes. I wondered if I was exposing the kids to too much. In retrospect, was it any worse than what I was exposing them to at home? That day, I missed work. We left the facility and went to the Marble Slab ice cream parlor. The peace I found at the ice cream parlor made me feel like I was on a vacation. The kids needed the getaway, and quite honestly, so did I.

The next day, we went to the Zoo with the shelter, and that was nice as well. It was good to see that other women were getting their lives together and witnessing their progress gave me hope. The kids were laughing, having fun, not afraid and just being kids. Refreshing as it was to feel a breakthrough of peace in the midst of our storm, we had to be cautious because not everyone at the shelter was an upstanding citizen or honest. I kept the kids really close to me, and believe me, that was hard when you find yourself in confined quarters with so many people. Most of my prized possessions were in the trunk of my car. During that time, I was still a graduate student and had a major paper due. I was living in a women's shelter, driving around with my computer in my trunk, missing work, the kids were missing school, and above all, we had no real address. How did I come to this?

The next day he called. An entire day passed before he even called to check on us. I spoke with him, and he was repentant. However, I was not convinced. I broke one of the most important rules of the safe house. I had lunch with him. I met with him at a local sandwich shop with the kids, and he cried as we left the restaurant. Still, I was not fazed, and that is when "it" happened. The pastor and wife of the church we attended called my cell phone. I didn't answer.

After several days, I finally spoke with them, and they asked me to go home. I told them that certain things needed to be in place before that happened. I needed some support from them to make sure that we would be safe and that my kids would get some counseling as well. They put things into place, and we went home. The church promised to counsel us as a couple and to get counseling for the kids. The kids never did get their counseling.

In the fall of 2000, I started to grow frightened of my husband again. This day, I had to go to an information-gathering session so that my son could attend a new school. We were looking into another school for him, and the meeting was mandatory. Additionally, there was a scheduled meeting for my husband to meet with a man regarding setting up a website for the business. Well, needless to say, I couldn't be two places at once, so I went to the meeting for my son. When the man arrived to meet about the website, my husband was upset because I was not there. It was just a few hours before he had to work the night shift, so he was tired, the children had messed up the living room, and he was frustrated.

Well, I expected him to be gone to work by the time I arrived home from my meeting, but that was not the case. When I arrived, I found him in the kitchen preparing his lunch for work. The children were already asleep. He began ranting and raging about the house not being clean. My reply to him was that it was clean when I left, and I could not control what happened once I left. He continued to be ugly until he left for work. A few days later, he apologized and stated to me that he knew he was wrong for arguing, but there was something in his head telling him to be mean to me and he could not help it. I started to think, "What would have happened if "it" would have told him to kill me or the kids? Would he have listened?" Now I am spooked! I had no family in Texas besides him and my kids.

Then there was the time I contemplated "it" meaning "no longer in the land of the living." I was plain 'ole tired, but I was more concerned about what my family would think if I left him. Would they think I was a failure? Would they say, "I told you so." Would they hate him? I never really wanted that to happen just in case we reconciled. I remember coming home from church, yes… church, and I was just plain tired. I didn't want to fight anymore, and in all honesty, I didn't have any fight left in me. I just wanted some peace of mind but could not find it anywhere.

Visualizing, if I just jumped out of the car and it rolled over me, I would not have to divorce him or live with him forever, let alone continue to deal with the constant ridicule and emotional pain. Then, God spoke to me in a still quiet voice and said, "Do not do it. What about the kids?" He said, "I love you". *"Come to Me, all who are weary and heavy-laden, and I will give you rest."* (Matthew 11:28) Hearing my Heavenly Father's voice was enough to get me through the day. If only we could focus on God's word and *"pray without ceasing"* (I Thessalonians 5:17), we would truly be all right.

Those who are contemplating suicide at this very moment, while you're reading this book, in the matchless name of Jesus, I pray that you would *take every thought captive and know that in your weakness, God's strength is made perfect* (2 Corinthians 12:9). Just hold on and I promise, tomorrow will get better. You will look back on today and think to yourself that God got you through it.

After we separated, my father finally found out what was going on. He never really cared for my husband. As a matter of fact, he didn't care for anyone that my sister, or I dated and ultimately married. He also found out that I had gone to a women's shelter and had taken the kids there. Needless to say, he was less than enthused. My family asked why I never told them about what was going on. Why I hadn't told them about how afraid I was, about the beatings that the kids got, or that I had been tired for a long time, on the brink of suicide, and the only answer I could come up with was, "I needed to cover his nakedness."

"Ham, the father of Canaan, saw the nakedness of his father, and told his two brothers outside but Shem and Japheth took a garment and laid it upon both their shoulders and walked backward and covered the nakedness of their father; and their faces were turned away, so that they did not see their father's nakedness." Genesis 9:22-23

I did not want to expose him. I kept thinking about how he had been raised, the unfortunate life situations that he had experienced in his life, and that he simply could not give to us what he did not have. Sounds familiar? He did not have the patience we needed. He did not have the compassion we desired. He did not have the gentleness we required. Nonetheless, regardless of his emotional incapacity, I now know that covering his nakedness, as Noah's sons did, was not applicable. I learned to guard my heart, my empathy and sympathy.

Sidebar

As a victim/survivor of molestation, domestic, and family violence who has overcome the abuse and working continuously to heal from the effects of trauma, it is never acceptable to remain in an abusive situation, let alone hide it. To do so weaves a web of danger that may result in continuous abuse of the victim, suicide, murder, murder-suicide, and any other form of oppression. With the astronomical increase of domestic violence and the affects thereof plastered all over the news, I realize that I should have told someone and sought help earlier, saving myself and my children from this traumatic experience.

Not long afterwards, we moved into our new home. I thought that moving into a new house would make us pretend that "it" was a home. Needless to say, that didn't last long. In June 2001, Tropical Storm Allison roared through Houston and I was sick as all get out that Friday night. My PCOS flared up causing excessive bleeding and cramping, necessitating that I may need to go to the emergency room. The cramping was so severe that it felt as though I was going through active labor. Anyway, it turned out that on this night in particular, the kids' bathroom was not clean enough for him. It was not up to military muster, and he was going to make it known. I was asleep and he entered our bedroom and began his usual ranting. It was about midnight, the kids were asleep, and I was as sick as a dog. I was still in graduate school and had class in the morning, so I was trying to get some rest amidst my pain. Inconsiderately, he kept fussing about the bathroom. When I figured out that he was not going to relent, I got out of the bed, doubled over in pain, and cleaned the bathroom. I did it because I did not want him to wake the kids up. If he had gotten them out of bed, it would have been a bad scene. After I finished cleaning the bathroom, he stated, "I didn't mean for you to clean it". What did he think was going to happen? I certainly was not going to allow him to badger the kids at midnight to clean a bathroom. It should have been able to wait until the morning. It was then that I thought to myself, "I gotta get out of here!"

Fighting Against the Odds

Chapter 13: The Second Time Around

We were in counseling again. At least this time, it was Christian counseling. Nevertheless, after many weekly sessions, little was accomplished. Just prior to our decision, okay, my decision, to separate, I found out what needed to be done to lose the weight, considering my health condition. Not trying to appease him anymore, I didn't even mention it, as my weight loss would be for me and only me. At that point, I had already lost over thirty-five pounds and recalled the minister that counseled us telling me that he noticed the weight loss and that I looked good. He asked my ex if he noticed, and he replied, "I guess it's hard to notice when you see someone every day." The counselor did not buy that for a moment and addressed it with him. "The very thing that you insisted was the source of your marital problems is being addressed, and you don't even notice?" Our problems were deeper than we thought.

By May 2001, we still had little to no progress in counseling. The minister stated, "Kim, maybe you just have to leave." This would be the second time that I had been told by a counselor to leave. This time I would listen. I spoke with my ex-husband and told him that we needed to improve by November, six months away, or I was leaving. Needless to say, he was not inspired to do anything. As a military man, he really did not like being forced to do anything, especially if it wasn't coming from a commanding officer, in his eyes. Maybe he didn't want to deal with his inner demons. Perhaps, we were getting closer to the truth in counseling than we thought. Only God knows.

The month of May brought no change. June, no change. July, no change. August, no change. September, no change. Then, "it" happened. My ex had an epiphany and realized that he had less than a month to get it together. He asked me, "Do you really want me to leave?" I replied, "What changes have been made at this point?" By now, we didn't even sleep in the same bedroom, and he hadn't desired to be with me intimately in almost a year. He told me that he would be okay living like that until our son turned eighteen. Our son was eleven years old! My response to that suggestion was, "The devil is a liar!" I could not subject myself to living like that anymore. It was not that I couldn't live like that; it was that I chose not to. I know better now.

November 1, 2001 was move out day. He moved as we had discussed. Six months ago, we talked about trying to work on the marriage so that this day would never have to happen. Approximately three to four weeks before he was to move out, he asked if I was serious about him leaving. I asked myself, "Is he serious?" He no longer wanted therapy and was not amenable to the therapy process. Nothing in the relationship had changed, and he wondered if I was serious. I could not have been more serious so, he went to live in his family's home.

Fighting Against the Odds

Chapter 14: On My Own

Several weeks after the separation, I was laid off from my job. I had been teaching at a charter school and worked in an administrative capacity. Staring uncertainty in the face, I thought, "He's still not coming back home."

For the first time in my life, I experienced peace in my home. No fussing, no belittling, no drama and thank God, no fear. Being a single parent for a long time now because he had not been a very active parent, was already familiar. Nonetheless, I was now finally at a place where I could breathe. I wasn't walking on eggshells and the kids began coming out of their shells. Although my son initially took the separation the hardest, he was not the one who experienced most of the beatings. It was my daughter who bared the brunt of his wrath. Naturally, he missed his father, but he did not have to be afraid anymore, at least not at home.

I truly do not want to make it sound like a cakewalk, as it wasn't. What I did not know was how difficult divorce would really be. Plain and simple, divorce is hard and God hates it. In the Hebrew language, the word "divorce" means (kawath - a primary root: to cut off, down or asunder; to destroy or consume, to be chewed, be destroyed, fail, be freed, hew (down), lose, perish utterly and want). I must be totally honest; I felt every one of those adjectives.

Financially, I struggled, and for a long time after the separation, the kids did act out. This whole thing was taking a toll on them as well. Solitude sometimes felt as though it would strangle me. Frankly, I did not know how to be "okay" in my singleness. New Year's Day 2002, I was alone. My son was with his father and my daughter had gone to a friend's house. I sat on the sofa watching, "Waiting to Exhale." I know… that was a brilliant selection! Well, after watching that movie, I felt worse. I put on my big black leather coat and decided to walk to the park, which was about four blocks from the house. I had to walk because the engine had just blown out in my car. I was now without transportation and still unemployed. However, I had a friend that was there for me that season. She would allow me to use her car to take my kids to school and to go job searching. She tried to be there for me, but I was in such a depression, I did not know how to allow her to help me. She offered to take me to her hometown in Clarksdale, MS for New Year's, but I declined. So, off to the park I went. It was really cold and just as I sat on the swing, it began to rain. I thought, is there any place of escape for me? Later on, I would learn that God wanted me to escape into His arms.

"But it is good for me to draw near to God; I have put my trust in the Lord God, that I may declare all Your works." Psalm 73:28

Fighting Against the Odds

Chapter 15: A Dream Deferred No Longer

Graduation approached. It was November 2nd or 3rd, and I prepared to take my comprehensive exam. Imagine having to take this exam while going through all this mess! Initially, I tried to take it on Halloween, go figure. After driving an hour in traffic, I arrived at the campus and realized that I had forgotten my driver's license at Randall's Supermarket. It was a Saturday when I took off to take my comprehensive exam for my first master's degree. In order to enter the Testing Lab, they required you to submit your license. The Friday before, I had gone to the grocery store, written a check, and forgot to get my license back after they requested it for I.D. So, I walked into the testing lab all ready to take my test, only to discover that I didn't have my license. I knew that if I went back to the market to get it, I would be late for my exam. So, I had to regroup, retrieve my license over the weekend, and took advantage of the impromptu extra time to study a bit more for my exam.

Monday, I was all set to take the test and was on pins and needles. Nervous, beyond nervous, knowing that the past two years would rest on this test. I did my best to regain my composure. We were allotted three hours to complete the exam, and I had to belt out at least nine pages to pass. So, here it goes. Within one and a half hours, I finished. I hit the Save button and lost all my information! One and a half hours, nine pages, and I was back to square one. The enemy was really on my tail. I composed myself, started all over, and still met the deadline with only three minutes to spare. GOD is good!

This graduation was so different from my undergraduate degree. You see, when I earned my bachelor's degree, I felt I had to make amends to my family for getting pregnant. I needed to show them that I was not just going to be a statistic. They did not tell me that, but that burdensome feeling during the pregnancy never left me. My teen pregnancy was one of the most isolating times of my youth. It was almost as isolating as the sexual abuse I suffered at the hand of my grandfather. I wrapped myself into my shame and wore it as if it were sack cloth and ashes. At the time, my mother had few words for me. This was not what she wanted for me. My father had only harsh, cruel, and bitter words for me, and those would sear into my memory and soul until adulthood. While obtaining my undergraduate degree, I found myself taking my report cards to my father to show him that I was doing well. In his nonchalant kind of way, he merely asked, "Are you going to law school after you graduate?" It would have done my heart good for him to simply say, even in a monotone way, "Good job!"

I graduated with my bachelor's at twenty-six years of age and was looking for validation from my father regarding a report card! Was I not "Shug" from "The Color Purple," as she wanted her father's approval once she married?

This Master's degree was for me! I had nothing to prove to anyone except myself and boy did it feel good! I was now starting to do things for myself and it was that first master's degree that led me to continue my expedition of learning.

Fighting Against the Odds

Chapter 16: A Tragic Mistake!

This season in my life got really hard. Once my ex-husband and I separated, I began to go out with a "friend". I trusted him and thought he cared about me. I would eventually learn that we had vastly different perspectives, values, and definitely disciplines. Here I was, separated, laid off from work and depressed, and what do I do? I "dated" someone battling depression, amongst other things. Talking about a double negative that does not turn into a positive. Often, when we were together, he drank to the point of intoxication and some occasions throwing up. It appeared that he self-medicated with alcohol. And he did so a lot. Calculating that his needs were greater than mine, he was not able to give me what I needed emotionally because he had his own issues to contend with.

Sidebar:

Alcohol tends to be the most common method of self-medication — as well as the most commonly abused substance since it's so widely available. It may be used to self-medicate stress, as well as depression and anxiety; though beer, wine, and liquor are all depressants and will therefore only make symptoms worse.

https://www.helpguide.org/articles/addictions/self-medicating.htm

Although we spent time going out to eat and listening to music at his home, I must say, he did not want to disrespect my home, considering I was not yet "officially" divorced. So, we never came to my house. It is funny that he would not want to disrespect my home, however, he disrespected me, and I allowed it.

His companionship was great for a while as he assisted me with job searches and the like. Well, I guess you can figure it out. It was not long before "it" happened. We fell into sexual sin and consequently, I became pregnant. When I told him that I was pregnant, his response was, "I thought you were on the pill." I was taken aback at the words that were coming out of his mouth. I took the liberty to remind him of the previous discussion we had when we were "just friends." I recall specifically explaining the details of my medical condition, which is why I wasn't on any birth control. I also discussed the fact that since my ex-husband, I had not been intimate with anyone, so there was no need to be on anything. Therefore, I know I made it very clear to him that I was not. Now, all of a sudden, he had selective amnesia. He went on to express his woes that a baby was the last thing he needed. You see, in August, he had just accepted his call into the ministry and this would tarnish his reputation and position at his church. Now, I was starting to see it was always all about him, his reputation, his position in ministry, and apparently his sexual appetite.

  Everything about me took a backseat to what would affect him with no concern for me. Here I was again being an emotional enabler, trauma bonding over depression, leaving me quandrafied. My rollercoaster of emotions kicked in with this probing question, "Did he ever care about me?" He NEVER asked what I wanted to do about the baby. It was simply understood that the pregnancy would be terminated. Unfortunately, I would terminate the pregnancy because life was just too difficult at that time for both of us. I was still unemployed, facing divorce, and just becoming a single parent of two children. What I remember most about that situation was the day of the procedure, I convalesced at his home for several hours. All I wanted was for him to hug or hold me, to comfort me and share in this loss. Nevertheless, we both lay in bed with our clothes on with our backs toward each other. I kept thinking to myself, "What have we done?" This one cost me BIG! Now, I had truly found my lowest point in life. I did not think anything could compare and yet, it got worse.

Upon terminating the pregnancy, we decided to start living how God wanted us to live, or so I thought. After all, he was a minister and I was trying to please God, which meant no more sex! That was a decision I was ready to abide by. On the contrary, our oaths and efforts of celibacy were short lived. One night, we were at his apartment listening to some music, the Isley Brothers in fact, and "it" happened again.

"Keep watching and praying that you may not enter into temptation; the spirit is willing but the flesh is weak." Matthew 26:41

He could not do it. He could not abstain, or he would not. While we were listening to music, he decided that he wanted to be romantic. I held him at bay as long as I could. I reminded him that we promised that we would not have sex anymore, but he proceeded to take my pants off. With no regard to the promise we made to God, he simply said, "Why are you teasing me?" I kept saying, "I thought we weren't going to do this anymore" but it was to no avail.

I was no match for him and felt like Ms. Celie in "The Color Purple" all over again. He crawled on top of me and did his business, leaving me feeling violated. I would later realize that my initial mistake was not going to his home, but rather answering the phone when he called.

As I began to write this book, I spoke with a friend of mine. She asked a very poignant question. "Why didn't you just say he raped you?" I had no reply. I blamed myself for that too. As a scratched record, I kept telling myself, "If I had not gone to his home, if I had not stayed so long, etc. it would not have happened."

"No temptation has overtaken you except such as is common to man; but God is faithful who will not allow you to be tempted beyond what you are able, but with the temptation will also make the way of escape, that you may be able to bear it."
I Corinthians 10:13

Reflecting on that situation, obviously I see a lot of things I could have done differently and acknowledged that I missed my way of escape. However, there is one thing that I truly had no power over, and that was his personal decision to override my will and violate me. I now know, that's on him. Desiring companionship does not equal sex, therefore forcing oneself on another is never acceptable. Many women have suffered in silence, the way I did, thinking just like I did, simply because we felt as though being sexually assaulted was our fault. At this stage of maturity in my life, I know what to take responsibility for and what not to.

Sidebar:

One in four women; that is 25 % of women and about 1 in 26 men have experienced completed or attempted rape. About 1 in 9 men were made to penetrate someone during his lifetime. Additionally, 1 in 3 women and about 1 in 9 men experienced sexual harassment in a public place.

https://www.cdc.gov/violenceprevention/sexualviolence/fastfact.html

Children and Teens: Statistics

Every 9 minutes child protective services substantiate or finds evidence for a claim of child sexual abuse.

- One in nine girls and 1 in 53 boys under the age of eighteen experience sexual abuse or assault at the hands of an adult.
- Child victims often know their perpetrator.

- Ninety-three percent are known to the victim.
- Seven percent are strangers.
- Fifty-nine percent are acquaintances.
- 34 % are family members.
- Eighty-two percent of all victims under eighteen are female.[4]
- Females ages 16-19 are four times more likely than the general population to be victims of rape, attempted rape, or sexual assault.[2]

The effects of child sexual abuse can be long-lasting and affect the victim's mental health. Victims are more likely than non-victims to experience the following mental health challenges:

- About four times more likely to develop symptoms of drug abuse
- About four times more likely to experience PTSD as adults

- About three times more likely to experience a major depressive episode as adults

https://www.rainn.org/statistics/children-and-teens

I really wanted to believe he cared. He even told me that he loved me enough to marry me and would love to be there for my children and me. After this fiasco, "Why would I think that he was capable of keeping promises, and more importantly, why would I want him to?" Maya Angelou wrote, *"When a person shows you who they are, believe them."*

"It is better to trust in the Lord than to put confidence in man."
Psalm 118:8

Quite honestly, had I looked at the termination of the pregnancy, and the sexual violation and focused on that, I would have been able to see immediately that he was not capable of loving anyone except himself. Needless to say, the marriage never occurred, and I can truly say that I thank God for that broken promise. God has so much greater for me. I have come to the realization that the man God will allow to find me will be equipped to cover me and the anointing on my life. He will be able to serve as a protector, prophet, provider, and priest.

Chapter 17: The Breaking Begins

"But He said to me, "My grace is sufficient for you, for My power is made perfect in weakness. Therefore, I will boast all the more gladly about my weaknesses, so that Christ's power may rest on me." 2 Corinthians 12:9

Shortly thereafter, I was watching Paula White on the television. At that time, I had NEVER seen a woman preacher before. I was captivated. On that day, she gave her testimony about being sexually abused, having self- esteem issues, and that her Father had committed suicide. I was glued to the television and made an appointment to watch her from then on, until I became employed.

As I prepared for an interview, I listened to CeCe Winan's, "Alabaster Box," and I began to just cry out to God, asking Him to help me. It was only His grace that kept me alive. Here I was, unemployed, going through a divorce and had an affair. Yes, it was an affair as I was not yet divorced! Just to mention those things in the same sentence with my name was heart wrenching. Nevertheless, I regained my composure, continued to prepare for the interview, and what do you know, I got that job. God then brought "it" to my remembrance… the discussion that I had with Him in the eighth grade. Dressing out for physical education class I said to myself, "I am going to be a nun when I grow up." Then the thought occurred, "Where did that come from?" I wanted purity so much that I thought that was the only way I was going to attain or recapture it. Now, I understand that I said "a nun" because I had never seen a woman preacher before. Several months later, I began Bible College and loved it!

This would be around the time another bomb would drop. I had not yet cut ties with the "minister" so he ended up introducing me to one of his friends. She and I hit it off well and still stay in contact with each other, to this day. Anyway, September 30th was his birthday and in my naivety, I assumed he and I would get together to celebrate his birthday, after he returned from visiting his daughter in Dallas, I must have been suffering from temporary insanity! Why would I still want to be with someone that could not or would not console me after their child was terminated and violated me? I must have really been in an exceptionally low place. He stated that he was tired from the drive and that he wanted to hang around the house and get some rest. He went on to tell me how the drive really took a lot out of him. Several days later, our mutual friend told me that she had spoken with him and that he had a date for his birthday. She was not aware that we had been dating. I thought I would die. I felt as though the wind was knocked out of me and for whatever reason, I did not immediately tell her about our dating.

The next day I called him and addressed it with him, and he confessed that it was true. I went on to say how we had promised each other that if we no longer wanted to be in this "relationship," we would tell one another. His reply was, "He didn't want to hurt me." I guess he did not think finding out like this would hurt. Heck, I do not think he really cared. I called him a lowlife in my thoughts. His lack of caring for me was so obvious even before this incident, but this one was the straw that broke the camel's back. Once again, why did I expect him to keep promises? Why was I still entertaining him? Stockholm syndrome, maybe? In all fairness to him, I had to be honest with myself and remembered that as we started dating, God brought me to the following passage of scripture:

"You are of your Father the devil, and you want to do the desires of your Father. He was a murderer from the beginning and does not stand in the truth because there is no truth in him. Whenever he speaks a lie, he speaks from his own nature, for he is a liar and the Father of lies." John 8:44

Now, am I calling him the devil? Certainly not! But the enemy used his carnality + my gullibility (derived from my past trauma, low self-esteem and loneliness) + both of our weaknesses against us both. He was not at a point spiritually to be honest or disciplined. God had already shown me the lack of integrity in him before we were ever involved. Still, once again, I needed to be loved so badly that I settled for any scraps that I could find.

"And He has said to me, "My grace is sufficient for you, for power is perfected in weakness. "Most gladly, therefore, I will rather boast about my weaknesses, so that the power of Christ may dwell in me." 2 Corinthians 12:9

Ironically, God will make you face your issues. Wouldn't you know it, the next semester, I had a class with him. Now, I must look at this joker's face every week and pretend that all is well. We were in a Christian institution pursing credentials of higher biblical learning and a greater moral compass. All I really wanted to do was to scream at everyone what a hypocrite he was. Oh, but that would make me one as well, so I had better put that rock down! "He who is without sin cast the first stone." *(John 8:7)* That stone would have boomerang back to me and knocked me out as well. So, I gathered my emotions and focused on what I was there to do.

We continued to attend the class and eventually he made his way up to my table. What was I supposed to do? I did what Jesus would have done. I functioned as if nothing was wrong and eventually, I was okay. Do not get me wrong, I was still hurting, but the soreness was starting to wear off. Over time, God would eventually heal me so that now there is just a scar. I often look at that scar to remind me of what I allowed myself to get into and what I have learned from it. We worked together and completed the class. By the fall, he was married to the woman that he had been dating. It would take a while for me to deal with that, especially since they now have a child together.

It has been about twenty years since I have seen him and quite honestly, I am okay. Recently, a mutual friend advised me that she saw him and his nephew. He and his nephew were on their way to get something to eat. My friend went on to say that she could smell the alcohol on his breath. I immediately had compassion for him and his family. After all this time, he is still battling the same demon. Therefore, I will

Dr. Kimberlyn Negret

continue to keep him and his family on my prayer list, for his total deliverance, and then God will really be able to use him.

Fighting Against the Odds

Chapter 18: Single For The First Time

I had never really been single before. When I had my daughter at age sixteen, I remained in my mother's home, finished school, and went on with life. When I left my mother's home, I got married and lived with my ex-husband and kids. So, I really didn't know what it was like to be single. Here I was thirty-five and single for the first time. Initially, it was harder than I thought it would ever be. Once the relationship with my "minister friend" was over, I had to deal with "me". Examining myself with God's Word, that I studied so emphatically, led me to the reasons I kept arriving at this same emotionally bankrupt place. Identifying why this "self-defeating" behavior was my default setting and the spirit I was carrying that attracted me to "it", was a "stronghold that needed to be broken.

Here I was, alone again but this time, I was determined to do it God's way. While in Bible College, I met someone who would later serve as a mentor in the ministry. We connected and I found out that she was forming a foundation to help the less fortunate. She held an event at her local church and invited me to speak. Me, speak? What have I to say? Well, it went off without a hitch and that was the start of me walking in my calling, although I didn't even know it.

Shortly thereafter, I met a pastor who happened to be single. Let's call him Jacob. Jacob and I hit it off well. I remember telling him that I had spoken at the event and his reply startled me. He said to me, "Kim, you know you preached a sermon, right?" My response was, "No, I had a talk with the people." He joked, "Your tennis shoes will run out before God does." As I tried to deflect from my calling, it always showed itself.

Within several months, I accepted my call in the ministry at his church and life was grand. Although it was apparent that we would not be dating, I truly began to enjoy his friendship and this new relationship with God. Now that I was a healthy student, I realized some of the valuable lessons I learned:

1. I am the apple of His eye, God that is.
2. How to share my feelings and trust others again.
3. Males and females can be platonic friends.
4. Everyone was not out to get me.
5. Someone can love you so much that they will stay away from you in lieu of hurting you.
6. "Pastors" are human too.
7. How to be an Intercessor.
8. The awesome cost of ministry - (time, talents, tithes, etc.).
9. To trust God more than ever before and totally depend on Him.
10. When unctioned by The Holy Spirit to do something, I realized that I don't have to know the details, just be obedient.

Once again, I had my bouts with loneliness and often wanted to escape back to New Orleans, but God would not release me, at least not then. There was a tug between my flesh and The Spirit as my flesh said, "Girl, go home and be with your family. It doesn't make sense to be here without anyone to have your back." The Spirit said, "Baby, just stay put as it is only a season." So, I stayed put and eventually the blessings that coincided with being single were revealed. The Apostle Paul states, in *I Corinthians 7:32-33*, *"But I want you to be without care. He who is unmarried cares for the things of the Lord—how he may please the Lord. [33] But he who is married cares about the things of the world—how he may please his wife."*

Paul is advising us to remain single if we can do so successfully and not burn with passions. He also indicates that we should count it a blessing to be single because we only have to concern ourselves with the Kingdom. On the contrary, if we are married, our loyalties then become divided as we assume responsibilities as a spouse. Therefore, trying to strike a balance between serving God and managing a household successfully is often a challenge.

Although, I still struggled with being alone, God never intended for us to feel alone. He did, however, want us to experience singleness, to live a life of being whole and complete with Him. I had not yet mastered the art of singleness which gave way to feelings of abandonment, always needing someone to be around, even if they didn't mean me any good. Seeking to be in the company of others gave me a false sense of security. I started to feel as though God had forgotten me. *"Eli, Eli, lama sabachthani?" that is "My God, My God, why have You forsaken Me?"* Matthew 27:46

At this point in my spiritual walk, I know God never leaves us nor forsakes us. Furthermore, I have learned to cherish the time I spend with the Him, making my heart overflow. I truly appreciate the quiet time with Him during prayer at night and the early mornings on the prayer line. During my current season of singleness, I relish in my time with Him. And if and when He sees fit to have me become a helpmate, I am certain God will be the center of our lives and the three-fold cord that binds us.

In June 2003, I was ordained as a minister, and my mother came to Houston to see me. She was so proud of me, and I was beaming with pride as well. I was finally doing "it" right. Although Jacob remained single for several more months, nothing transpired between us but the neutral companionship I needed. He always maintained respect for me, and for that I am eternally grateful.

"For all those things My hand has made, and all those things exist," says the Lord. "But on this one will I look: On him who is poor and of a contrite spirit, and who trembles at My Word." (Isaiah 66:2) Surrendering my will, allowing God to become my greatest comfort and company, began to fill every void in ways I couldn't image. I would later learn more of the promises of God and the true gift of singleness.

Chapter 19: The Other Face of Ministry! Jezebel Is In the House!

"But I have this against you, that you tolerate the woman Jezebel, who calls herself a prophetess, and she teaches and leads my bond-servants astray so that they commit acts of immorality and eat things sacrificed to idols." Revelation 2:20

Who was she and how did Jezebel get in? This is what I had to ponder. I also had to learn to trust the gifting inside of me. Our ministry was a new one and my pastor did not yet know that he had the gift of prophecy. What we must understand about the spirit of Jezebel is that it wants to come against prophetic ministries in an attempt to shut up the "mouth of God" or simply stated, what God has to say. I understood the gifting on his life and attempted to fight this Jezebel spirit. However, I was in the fight by myself. Jezebel is a master spirit, in which it controls the ground troops of Satan. We must recognize that military operations are very methodical and organized, and it had done its homework.

Jacob and I were very close. We talked about almost everything. Things were going really well for a while and then "it" happened. It was Father's Day, 2003 and we were in fellowship at another church. There was a praise dancer there and she caught my pastor's eye. Shortly thereafter, I knew that we would be in a fight for our lives. Before this young lady ever entered our church, her mother came in and scoped it out like a vulture. She was coming to ensure that their work of seduction (manipulation) would be accomplished, and the environment was right for the picking. Just a few short weeks later, the young lady re-appeared and that is when all Hades broke out.

She and Jacob began to date and literally all hell cut loose. I am not certain why the young lady did not like me, but she made it obvious. Jacob used to call me his "Nathan" because I would always let him know what God was telling me and at one time, he actually appreciated the gift. I later found out that I was not the spirit of Nathan, but Elijah, with the sword in my mouth. Well, things took a shift, and not for the better. Eventually she began attending the church. My life was in turmoil every time I entered the church.

I contacted Jacob and told him what I thought of his relationship with this woman and initially, he was receptive. The next day "it" happened. He went totally off on me. He snapped! I had known this man for a while and never saw him act like this. I was bewildered! This was not the man that I had grown to respect, revere, and love. IT WAS NOT! This would be the first of two really horrible arguments that we would have.

Jacob told me that if I didn't leave his business alone, I would never preach in the church again. I remember shouting, "You can stop me from preaching in your pulpit, but you can't stop me from preaching the gospel. I'll preach it on the streets with a bull horn, but I'll keep preaching." *Romans 8:30 says, "And these whom He predestined, He also called; and these whom He called, He also justified; and these whom He justified, He also glorified."*

Two weeks prior to the young lady joining our church, I was invited to attend a seminar at a church I attended on Sunday mornings. The other church would eventually become my church home. The seminar lecture that morning was entitled, "Demonology" and it was there that I was introduced to seducing spirits. This spirit was called Jezebel! Now, geared with that information, how do I tell Jacob this about the love of his life? An internal battle began as I was at war with myself on how to respond to this devil in a church dress. I armed myself with every piece of material that I could read regarding this spirit. I knew that we were in big trouble. No one else at the church could see what I saw.

During that time, the prophetic gift upon my life became more evident. God would allow me to know just when something was going to happen. He would allow me to know when Jacob was in danger and where the attack would come from. Quite honestly, God would allow me to know dates, times, and the particulars of an incident.

It was the church anniversary, and I was there with my two kids. Although we had other ministers on staff, they could not care less about me at this point. They understood that Jacob was upset with me and it was in their best interest to stay away from me, so I was" persona non grata"; in Latin that literally means "an unwelcome person." Jacob and I were not on speaking terms because I had told him what God had told me about his relationship with this woman, and he was furious with me.

"Even my own familiar friend in whom I trusted, who ate my bread, has lifted up his heel against me." Psalms 41:9

For over a month, he did not speak with me. I was totally ignored by him in church. The other staff ministers were ambivalent as well. Here I go again. The one true friend that I thought I had has now turned on me and I am alone again. Not only that, but I couldn't even worship at church in peace.

As time passed, Jacob and I resumed our friendship; however, it just wasn't the same. I walked on eggshells all the time. I was always concerned about what he would think if I told him what God was telling me about his relationship with this young lady. Understand, I was not jealous, for he dated other women before, and believe me, other women were interested! This relationship was different. This relationship was designed to kill his integrity, his testimony, his ministry, and ultimately, to kill him. How was I to convey this to him without looking like I was crazy? After all, it had just been a few weeks prior that he totally went off on me. Needless to say, I didn't want to invite that wrath down on me again. However, when God gives a prophet something to do, they are to do it! In *1 Samuel 15*, you will find that the Prophet Samuel was sent by the Lord to anoint Saul as the king over His people. Samuel instructed Saul as to what he was supposed to do and why he should do it. Samuel gave very detailed and precise instructions to Saul in regard to destroying Amalek for what he had done to Israel. However, Saul did it his own way and ultimately lost the kingdom.

Samuel said, *"Has the Lord as much delight in burnt offerings and sacrifices in obeying the voice of the Lord? Behold, to obey is better than sacrifice, and to heed than the fat of rams. for rebellion is as the sin of divination, and insubordination is as iniquity and idolatry. Because you have rejected the word of the Lord, He has also rejected you from being king."* 1 Samuel 15:22-23

Therefore, I continued to tell him what God was telling me and as time went by, I grew less fearful. Time went by and Jacob and I still got along despite the confusion with his new fiancé. I was then serving as Assistant Pastor, and on this particular Wednesday, I was to lead a Bible study. I remember that for a while it was just the four of us: Jacob, the other assistant pastor, his fiancé and me. It was revealed that the other co-pastor and his fiancé were planning something for the young ladies at the church and had purposely left me out of the planning. When Jacob got wind of it, he shut the entire thing down. He addressed it at this meeting, and when I found out how they really felt about me, I was crushed. I must say, on this occasion he did defend me and that felt great. Later, I would learn that this experience would only be training ground for me in ministry.

I learned to have "a face of flint." *"For the Lord God will help Me; Therefore, I will not be disgraced; Therefore, I have set My face like a flint, And I know that I will not be ashamed. He is near who justifies Me; Who will contend with Me? Let us stand together. Who is My adversary? Let him come near Me. surely the Lord God will help Me; Who is he who will condemn Me? Indeed, they will all grow old like a garment; the moth will eat them up. Who among you fears the Lord? Who obeys the voice of His Servant? Who walks in darkness and has no light? Let him trust in the name of the Lord and rely upon his God."* Isaiah 50:7-10

If the enemy knew that he could get to me with people talking about me, lying on me, or just being ugly to me, I would be in BIG trouble.

"If you have run with footmen and they have tired you out, then how can you compete with horses? If you fall down in a land of peace, how will you do in the thicket of the Jordan?"
Jeremiah 12:5

I needed to pass this test. I threatened to leave the church several times but stayed and somehow believed that it was going to get better. It never did. Pastor had gotten engaged, and his new fiancé didn't like the fact that I was part of the ministry.

I then enrolled in a course at a local church. I really needed to be around some positive saints! I signed up for "Purity with Purpose". That course changed my life. The lessons I gleaned, molded and shaped the course of my life forever. This course taught me about purpose and destiny, and that God had one for me! The meaning of my name (Kimberlyn) derived from a royal family, and meant seeker of truth, chief common ruler, one of honor, refreshing spirit. Kimberly is also a place in South Africa located near Cape

Good Hope. This revelation of origin was so emotional for me that I fell to the floor in the class and began crying. I always had a passion to go to Africa to help with abandoned babies and those starving. So, to find out that my name was tied to Africa was too much for me to handle. Essentially that course changed my course.

"The Spirit of the Lord GOD is upon me, Because the LORD has anointed me To bring good news to the afflicted; He has sent me to bind up the brokenhearted, To proclaim liberty to captives And freedom to prisoners; To proclaim the favorable year of the LORD And the day of vengeance of our God; To comfort all who mourn, To grant those who mourn {in} Zion, Giving them a garland instead of ashes, The oil of gladness instead of mourning, The mantle of praise instead of a spirit of fainting. So they will be called oaks of righteousness, the planting of the LORD, that He may be glorified." Isaiah 61:1-3

Other lessons that I learned were understanding purpose, biblical, and historical perspectives of women. "Who are you and why are you, you?" I learned about spiritual gifts, keys to building happy and holy relationships, male and female differences, building a hedge and breaking soul ties, letting go of the past, and consecration. I now had the keys to live a successful single life. THANK GOD!

Needless to say, once the devil found out that I was taking this course, an imp was dispatched. Let's call him Adam. I had been working with Adam and we became friends. We would play tennis together, go walking together, and hang out. He was married. I rationalized it because, initially, he had invited his wife to come with us. Later, I'll get to the real reason that I started to hang out with him. Anyway, the culmination of the class was a wedding ceremony. At this ceremony, the graduates made a vow to God that we would remain pure and walk in our purpose and destiny. Well, I hadn't remained pure prior to the finalization of my divorce, but I was certainly going to walk in my purpose and destiny now. From that day on, I would walk in purity and bless God. I have been doing it ever since.

So, why did I hang out with Adam? I must be totally honest with you and myself. It was because I still had feelings of lingering loneliness. As God tried to protect me in a little box, I took myself out of that box and began to hang out with Adam. Emotional ties were formed as I became accustomed to spending time with Adam. It would only lead to pain and misery. It was fun for a while. We played tennis together, ate out together, talked for hours on end. He was quite handy too. God began to make it real clear that I was heading into dangerous waters and that I needed to don a life preserver, so I did. I ended the friendship and have not spoken with him in years.

"Therefore, since we have so great a cloud of witnesses surrounding us, let us also lay aside every encumbrance and the sin which so easily entangles us, and let us run with endurance the race that is set before us." Hebrews 12:1

Dr. Kimberlyn Negret

Shortly thereafter, a minister friend of mine invited me to attend T.D. Jakes', "God's Leading Ladies: Life Enrichment Program". I wondered if I should really travel four and a half hours each way, every other Saturday and pay $500.00 to attend this class? Is this really what God was asking of me? Then "it" happened. The Holy Spirit told me to invest in myself, so I did. I learned so much and experienced so much, and I am eternally grateful for both programs.

Fighting Against the Odds

Chapter 20: A Prophetic Encounter

The first prophecy given to me was at a Prophetic conference in Oklahoma City, Oklahoma. Three of us traveled to the conference for the time of our lives, and the three-day conference and information gathered there was invaluable. The first day of the conference started with prophecy going out over those in attendance. A prophet came up to our group and asked, "Who was the writer in the group?"

I didn't say anything initially, however, God brought to my memory a children's book that I started when I lived in New Orleans. I acknowledged I was the one, and she stated that God would use me to write books. Go figure. Another prophet approached me that day with further reveal. Prior to attending this conference, I was praying for the gift of healing. I regularly visited Texas Children's Hospital's Neonatal Intensive Care Unit or NICU for short. I signed up to volunteer to hold critically ill infants. These infants were hospitalized long-term while their parents returned to work. It helped the babies, nurses, parents, and quite honestly, it helped me. The

Prophet lifted my left hand and gently grasped my left ring finger. She went on to tell me that I would be used to heal cases of AIDS, cancer and other illnesses, and that all I would have to do was to speak the Word and it would happen. Now, I know this sounds great, however, on that day, I was not ready, nor did I want to hear this. You see, when she reached for my hand, more specifically the ring finger, I immediately thought she was going to prophesy that I was about to get married, and when she didn't, I was disappointed. Yes, I know that sounds shallow, but I didn't quite know how to appreciate the gifting on my life at that time. God had just answered a prayer, and I had the nerve to be disappointed!

The conference continued and we learned a lot. On the last day of the conference, we began discussing dreams. I thought, "I am in the clear. No more "prophecy" or so I thought. I walked into the sanctuary, unassumingly, and took a seat. The prophet then looked at me and began speaking. I thought to myself, certainly he is not speaking to me. I came to hear about the dreams, enough already about the prophecy.

I was in overload mode. He told me that I had been hurt by the church. What I didn't know was that he was prophesying about the future. He went on to say that I preferred being in the background, which was certainly true. Then he went on to say that God would bring me to the forefront and I was not at all comfortable with hearing those words. I left the conference knowing that I still had so much to learn, but more importantly, so much more to give. God had given me several prophecies regarding "The Power of Forgiveness."

"Be kind to one another, tender-hearted, forgiving each other, just as God in Christ also has forgiven you." Ephesians 4:32

As defined by Webster's Standard Dictionary, forgiveness means to pardon; to overlook. It was now my turn to forgive those who hurt me and it was the only way that God could use me to further the Kingdom. Considering all the hurt I endured, I knew this would be a challenge. It happened right before my ordination, and I was fighting "it". My grandfather, the abuser, was in the hospital and God told me to call him and ask about his salvation. I thought to myself, God, You can't be serious! I was in the tub and I audibly heard God say again, "Call him."

"Now the word of the Lord came to Jonah the son of Amittai, saying, "Arise, go to Nineveh, that great city, and cry out against it; for their wickedness has come up before Me." But Jonah arose to flee to Tarshish from the presence of the Lord. He went down to Joppa and found a ship going to Tarshish; so he paid the fare, and went down into it, to go with them to Tarshish from the presence of the Lord." Jonah 1:1-3

So, I called my mother to get the number to the hospital, and then I called him. I asked how he was doing, and he said, "Not too bad." He acted as though he had never done anything to me. I figured that answer was good enough, so I ended the conversation. I got back into the tub and God said,

"You didn't do what I told you to do! I told you to ask about his salvation".

I got right out of the tub and called him back, this time to ask if he was saved. His response was, "Yes." It was weird because I felt truly happy that he was saved. I didn't even want to see him go to hell.

The day of my ordination was also a day of healing for my mother. I told my two sisters about the abuse, and it appears that one of them leaked it out to my mother. The morning after the ordination, my mother approached me and asked me about it. Because God had dealt with me and my forgiving my grandfather, I was able to help my mother with her unforgiveness as well. I told her about it with as little detail as possible. It just wasn't necessary. I then told her to forgive him because I had. She cried, I consoled her and then I went off to church. There was no reason to continue lamenting over that which God had healed. It was time to move on.

God certainly has a way of cleansing you. Hurricane season 2004 came about and my family needed to flee from

New Orleans. I couldn't believe it. I allowed my grandfather to come to my home. I lived in a two-bedroom apartment, and I gave up my bedroom to him without question, for he was truly ill and fragile. The anger was finally gone.

Several short months later, I received a call while at work. It was my daughter on the phone, telling me that he was dead by suicide. My grandfather committed suicide. He ended all his pain. Throughout the years, God showed me the pain that he lived with. Having lost both of his parents as a small child, not having much stability, being abused himself, and experiencing bouts of depression, he too, was a victim. The physical ailments along with the harshness of life became too much for him and he ended it, just like that. I fell to the ground and prayed for his soul. Imagine that, praying for the person who catapulted me into a life of promiscuity and fear, and now I prayed for him. What an awesome God we serve!

Now it was time to let my ex-husband go. Shortly after the divorce, we had several conversations about what had gone wrong during our marriage. To be totally honest, our marriage should have never occurred. For a while after the divorce, I felt as though God was punishing me for leaving. Some might believe that I deserved it, but God is a loving and merciful God. He has forgiven me, and I've forgiven my ex-husband. Now don't get me wrong, it was a process, and a lengthy one. Most importantly, I have forgiven myself.

Fighting Against the Odds

Chapter 21: More Forgiveness

The Aftermath of Hurricane Katrina

Now, I had to forgive my father and let go of the hurt associated with the abandonment I felt from my childhood. As I stated before, he could not give what he didn't have or had not learned... or so I thought. It was August 27, 2005, peak hurricane season. Hurricane Katrina was on the way. I received a call from my sister, telling me that they would be evacuating New Orleans because Katrina was heading toward them. The family loaded into the car and made haste to Katy, Texas. My son, granddaughter, and I eagerly awaited them as they journeyed. What usually took six- and one-half hours became a twelve to fifteen-hour drive. They arrived at 2:30 a.m. Sunday morning. What they thought would be our normal two to three day "hurri-cation" would turn into an event that would eventually be noted in history as one of the headlines of the century. It would also raise questions regarding how the government was equipped to handle catastrophic events.

Two months prior to Hurricane Katrina, I purchased my home. Normally, you would find me, my son, and our cat "Elmo", lovingly known as boo-boo kitty, hanging around or putting something on the grill. Well soon, the dynamics of our household would change. The house now sheltered eight people, a cat, and a dog. The only person missing was my father. He opted to stay back in New Orleans. As you probably already know, many older people from New Orleans would typically stay put during hurricanes and hope for the best. Well, around 10:15 a.m. Sunday morning, we contacted my father, and he assured us that he was going to evacuate to Baton Rouge. Usually, this was an hour and a half trip, but the trip took him over twelve hours this time. He would not be able to make it to Texas. As the hurricane pummeled through New Orleans, he braved the hurricane from his car. There were no hotel rooms left in Baton Rouge, but if he didn't stay put, he would find himself stranded, so he stayed in the parking lot of a hotel as the hurricane passed.

Dr. Kimberlyn Negret

My father wasn't really good with remembering numbers, so he wrote our cell phone numbers down on a piece of paper. Well, during the hurricane the slip of paper got wet and consequently destroyed the telephone numbers. He had no way to contact us and we couldn't contact him. For a week, we watched, along with the rest of the world, the devastation taking place in New Orleans. Although we tried to remain optimistic and positive, it became increasingly difficult. Father was a pretty independent person, and we thought that in lieu of staying in traffic, he would venture back home and brave the hurricane in New Orleans, that or evacuate to the Superdome. There were very disturbing stories circulating about the state of the city, and we didn't know what to believe. I recall leaving work early because the stress of not knowing the whereabouts of my father was almost too much to bear. As I drove home, I became overwhelmed and began sobbing uncontrollably. I pulled over to the side of the road and attempted to contact a Congressperson here in Texas, begging her to send help to New Orleans. People who survived the hurricane were now dying from heat exhaustion, lack of medical attention, facilities, and basic food and water. New Orleans now looked like a third world country. This was my hometown plastered on the television and we looked like Somalians. My family in Houston and the rest of the world watched in horror.

The Lord says, "He won't put more on you than you can stand...." I served as a board member for a local ministry in Houston and because of that, my biography could be found on the internet. My father arrived safely in Baton Rouge and finally found a room. He mentioned to some people in the hotel that he was trying to locate us in Katy, Texas. They assisted him on the internet and after some research, he found my telephone number and finally contacted us. This was only God. I had not been home an hour before I received a call from my father stating that he was okay. I remember the call like it was yesterday. When I heard his voice, I said, "Daddy, is that you?" and he said, "Yes." My mother and two sisters wept. God answers prayers. Daddy went on to tell us the details of his journey, or adventure if you will. Our relationship would forever be changed.

As for New Orleans itself, it will NEVER be the same. Recently, I went home to assess the damage again. I went there earlier in the year to visit with my friend just prior to her death. It looked the same - blighted homes and despair on the faces of so many of the people. As we could expect, some people were still very angry about all of the chaos and trauma they suffered. So, it wasn't the same at all.

I visited with one of my mother's neighbors for a very brief time and I left somewhat broken, but hopeful. As she answered the door of her trailer, she was very happy to see me, and the feeling was mutual. She was okay, considering all that she had been through. She was hopeful and quite elated to know that family members would possibly move back into my mom's house. She had hope for her old neighborhood, although many others had no glimmer of such.

I visited all the homes that I lived in as a child; 2404 Deers Street, 2636 North Johnson, and 2419 Franklin Avenue.

At the time of my visit, all were abandoned… memories dear and not so dear came flooding back to me. Uncertainty resided with those memories, not knowing if all my neighborhood friends made it out as well as my other family, was disturbing. Several of the homes were just gone, torn down. The sandwich shops in my old neighborhood closed down. Lawns were overgrown, buildings boarded up and people were still looking lost. Then, I went to 2212 Annette Street. That was the spot where our family met every holiday. This was my father's childhood home and that of my great-grandfather, Phillip Johnson. He was a minister, and I always recall seeing him with his Bible, reading. Then there was "Big Mama", my great-grandmother. She, too, was a praying woman. I remember walking through the house, and she would "catch you." We all knew what that meant---she would then minister to you. We would often try to get past her, but there was no passing her by. She was a strict disciplinarian, and she didn't play. Most of all, she was a prayer warrior. We reminisced how, as children, we spent countless hours there with numerous generations. So, as my sister and I got out of the car, those fond memories dissipated as we were grief-stricken at the site of our family house. Now, the home that had been in the family for decades was now a mere frame, a skeleton, and had no life left. I understood the loss of sparkle in my father's eyes. He made it through the storm…or had he? Physically he survived, but mentally and emotionally, he was still battling the winds and the waves, which subsequently carried him to a new place within himself. The father I had was now much different.

In December 2006, I received my first birthday present from my father and it was a gold cross pendant with diamonds on it. I cherished that pendant because he had given it to me.

In June 2007, as I recuperated from surgery, my father suffered a stroke, yet he recovered well. For the first time in his life, he was taking the directions of the doctors and physically, he looked better but somehow, his spirit was still heavy. I continued to pray for his strength and peace of mind. Most disturbing to me during this visit was that the shine in my father's eyes was gone. It seemed as if every drop of joy had been sucked out. The toxicity: that is the despair, frustration, and the uncertainty, of the environment was taking its toll. As with life, that was only a season. My father picked himself up by his bootstraps and started a new legacy for himself and the family.

Chapter 22: Forgiveness 2.0

"But if you do not forgive men their trespasses, neither will your Father forgive your trespasses." Matthew 6:15

December 2006 would bring another tough test. My daughter was getting married, and her biological father would be attending. Now, I must admit, I hadn't really worked on forgiveness with him. I thought, "Out of sight, out of mind." Not so, said God. I needed to forgive him in my heart and make this one of the best days of my daughter's life. That is exactly what I did. I made sure that he had a "Father/Daughter" dance, and sat he and his wife at the table along with my daughter. Her half-sister was in the wedding and we had a wonderful time. Once again, God is good and is always right.

That year, I also lost my best friend of 25 years. She was battling cancer. Two years prior, I received a call from her and she told me that she had breast cancer. We prayed and believed in her total healing. She was fine for two years and then it happened again. The cancer was back. This time, the cancer had spread to her brain. I was devastated. God told me to catch a plane to New Orleans to visit with her, pray for her, speak with her family, and to give her communion, so I did. I packed CDs, Bibles, anointed oil, and anything else I thought would help. Several weeks later, I got the call that she passed away. I thought to myself, "Was I not consecrated enough? What had I done wrong?"

God then answered me in a still quiet voice. "I sent you as a minister of reconciliation as you were to reconcile her back to Me."

"For HE Himself is our peace, who made both groups into one and broke down the barrier of the dividing wall, by abolishing in His flesh the enmity, which is the Law of commandments contained in ordinances, so that in Himself He might make the two into one new man, thus establishing peace, and might reconcile them both in one body to God through the cross, by it having put to death the enmity." Ephesians 2:14-16

Dr. Kimberlyn Negret

I found that God's Word is true. Before He takes away from you, He will add. I thank God that He brought my other friend back just in the nick of time. Jacob was able to help me through what I thought would be one of the hardest times of my life, the loss of my long-time friend. At the same time, I had gotten a report from the doctor stating that I needed to have a hysterectomy. This was devastating news to me, because I still held out hope that the right person would come along, and I would have one more child. I had to come to terms with the abortion that I had several years prior. I always prayed for three children and God had given me three, but I killed the third. Be that as it may, I had to get off my bed of affliction and stop allowing the enemy to torment me with my past. God in His infinite grace and mercy forgave and restored me. Now, I needed to forgive myself.

"There is therefore now no condemnation to them which are in Christ Jesus who walk not after the flesh, but after the Spirit." Romans 8:1

I arrived at the hospital armed with my Bible, headphones, and my CD case. I listened to Juanita Bynum-Weeks', "He's A Wonder and I Don't Mind Waiting", repeatedly. I found strength in that. It was during this time that God spoke to me regarding the book. He told me, "Write." I was convalescing at my mother's home, and planned to just watch television and lay around. I needed this six-week break. However, God spoke to me again, after one week of recuperation and said, "That's enough time off, get back to work".

Jacob called me and stated that God wanted to have some quality time with me. I knew that God had given him that message. With pillows on the floor and my face in the carpet, I started my prayers, worship, and devotionals again. Just as Jesus was tempted after His time of consecration, two imps had been dispatched to see if I had secured some areas of my life. Imp Number One appeared from the past. The person that I hung out with after being hurt by Jacob, left a message for me stating that he heard that I was in the hospital and was just checking on me. We had some mutual friends and they called to see if I had gotten his message. I advised them that, indeed, I had received his message, but that chapter of my life was over. He was no longer with his wife, and honestly, I prayed that God would restore that marriage. I forgave him, and God certainly had forgiven me. We had nothing else to talk about.

Imp Number Two was a more recent demon. Last summer, I met a man as I taught summer school, and he appeared cool. He was engaged to be married in November 2006 so, we emailed photographs back and forth, as my daughter was getting married in December 2006. I prayed for him, his fiancé, and his family. It appeared innocent enough. We talked every couple of months. I advised him that I was having surgery and wanted him to keep me in his prayers. He told me that he had been really stressed out by his new responsibilities as a new husband, new stepfather, and dealing with in-laws. I prayed with, and for him, and he commented that he felt better after speaking with me. Okay, call me naive, but I really thought he was talking about my prayers for him.

I got a call the day after my surgery, and he sounded sort of strange. I thought to myself, maybe it was my medication, so I just dismissed it. Approximately two weeks later, I got a call at 7:10 in the morning. I thought it must be really important for someone to be calling so early. I was already up at 5:10 for morning prayer, worship, and devotionals. We talked for a while, and then I realized that he was not at work. He was calling me from home. It was his six-month anniversary. He went on to say that he sounded so strange when he called me at the hospital, because he wanted to visit me and send me flowers. He clearly knew that was not appropriate. He then disclosed that if he had met me three months earlier, he would never have gotten married to his wife. He went on to say that I was the type of woman he was attracted to. He said that he liked professional women with a light complexion. I wondered, "What the heck is going on?" Here I was under the impression that I was helping this brother and he had a totally different agenda. Then I got mad! As we concluded the conversation, I got a call from Jacob - perfect timing! I got off the phone with Imp Number Two and advised Jacob of what had just taken place. As I've stated previously, I always try to "consider my own ways" as stated *in Haggai 1:7*. Examining myself, I contemplated, "Did I do anything to lead this person on? I know that I didn't entertain any inappropriate conversations with him. Where had I gone wrong?" Jacob assured me that it was not my issue but the man's issue totally. From then on, I have not spoken with him.

CAUTION: We must ALWAYS protect the anointing on our lives! Once you realize there is a calling on your life, you must know that the enemy knows it as well.

"It" just got tougher. In June 2007, God turned the heat up. I was preparing to speak at our church's Single's Conference when God began dealing with me. He told me that He could see the little parts of pain, the lack of forgiveness, and insecurity that I had been hiding. I thought I conquered those things, but He showed me otherwise. Although I resumed the friendship with Jacob, I had not totally forgiven him. I was still afraid to share and be "genuinely/authentically me" because I feared being hurt or rejected again. He preached for one of our Bible studies, and the topic was, "Stretched for what's next." He used *Joshua 3:5* as an example, *"Then Joshua said to the people "Consecrate yourselves, for tomorrow the Lord will do wonders among you."*

To consecrate myself would mean letting go of the past hurts and forgiving him fully. I must admit, I didn't know how to let "it" go. I wanted to, but I just didn't know how. I would need God's help with that. At the end of Bible study that night, I got on the altar and waited for God to work with me. Getting on the altar is when a person either kneels or lays across the altar and prays. This is a time when you pour your heart out to God and remain there until you feel He has heard your petition and you have received resolution or peace with the petitions made. It is also a place where you can just go to commune with God. I'm not saying that this is the only place where this can occur, but on this day, that is what I did.

I was already fasting and had been fasting for about a month when God revealed this to me, so I increased my fast to the Daniel Fast. During my quiet time with the Lord, He told me that where He was leading me, I couldn't take my baggage with me. So, He continued to show "me" to myself. God has shown me that if I can't forgive and totally release people, I would just take all of my hurts, insecurities, and pains into my next marriage and ministry. I knew that was not God's will for my life. Therefore, I allowed myself to be placed on the potter's wheel, just as Jeremiah did.

"The word which came to Jeremiah from the Lord, saying: "Arise and go down to the potter's house, and there I will cause you to hear My words." Then I went down to the potter's house, and there he was, making something at the wheel. And the vessel that he made of clay was marred in the hand of the potter; so he made it again into another vessel, as it seemed good to the potter to make. Then the word of the Lord came to me, saying: "O house of Israel, can I not do with you as this potter?" says the Lord. "Look, as the clay is in the potter's hand, so are you in My hand, O house of Israel!"
Jeremiah 18:1-6

Fighting Against the Odds

Chapter 23: The Jezebel Spirit: More Learning

I received confirmation that another battle was about to begin. One night after Bible study, I got a call from my mother. She advised me that Bishop John Francis was on Trinity Broadcast Network (TBN). I tuned in and was astonished. He was talking about the spirit of Jezebel. We tuned into the last two minutes of the program. I was intent on catching it again, so I left my television on TBN for the better part of the next day. Two and a half months earlier, I purchased two books regarding the same subject. Francis Frangipane titled one book, *"The Jezebel Spirit"* and the other book was, *"Confronting Jezebel: Discerning and Defeating the Spirit of Control"*, by Dr. Steve Sampson. The Jezebel Spirit arrived at my home approximately one week after I ordered it. As Bishop Francis spoke with Archbishop Duncan Williams, my spirit quickened that I had not received *"Confronting Jezebel."* The next morning, my ex-husband came over to pick up my son. They were going to do a furniture delivery, and he gave my son a package for me. I took the package and placed it on the floor and then it hit me. This is the book! I opened the package and sure enough, the book had arrived. I asked my ex-husband how long he had the book and he confessed that he had it for a while. I still can't explain why the book went to his house.

Later that day "it" happened again. I was preparing to go to minister with someone when TBN came on. It was the rebroadcast of the Jezebel program. This time, I was able to catch it from the beginning. Divinely, one of the special guests was the author of the book I had received that very morning! I must add that I don't believe in coincidences. It all began to make sense to me. I had been anointed to recognize this spirit.

I thought to myself, now Jacob has finally gotten it. He also recognized the Jezebel spirit that once lived in him and inhabited his now ex-wife. Four years after I was frightened to death to tell him what God told me; he could now see for himself. It was God's timing and revelation. Now, how do I encourage him to stay focused? All that God was doing inside of him, all that God was doing through him, and all that God has destined for him, that was what he was to focus on. God had taken him through a metamorphosis, and he had truly been tested in the Fruit of the Spirit.

"But the fruit of the Spirit is love, joy, peace, longsuffering, kindness, goodness, faithfulness, gentleness, self-control. Against such there is no law." Galatians 5:22

He was now becoming the person that God always wanted him to be and subsequently the person he always wanted to be. After almost ten years of friendship, again he was there for one of the most difficult times of my life. Because I was residing in New Orleans and he lived in Houston, he often visited with my mother as she neared the end of her journey. He would spend time with her, encouraging her to eat, administering communion, praying for her, and giving me updates. His care for Mom allowed me to function in New Orleans until we could get her home. For all his time and love for my mom, I am eternally grateful.

Dr. Kimberlyn Negret

Chapter 24: Can These Dry Bones Live?

While I ministered at my previous church, we often fellowshipped with another local church. Once I left that assignment, I joined that church. From 2005 until 2010, I served faithfully. I loved my church. My family loved the church. Five generations of my family worshipped God in this church. He was there every time my mother was hospitalized. He blessed our homes. The Bishop was my pastor. He was my spiritual Father. How could this happen? Why is this happening to me again? Can I recover from this? At the time, five generations were depending on me to make the right decision and this weed of distraction pops up.

I finally decided to try the "dating thing" again, after all, it had been years. I hadn't had much time to focus on dating because I was busy in ministry. I served as a Youth Pastor, Elder over the Singles and Altar Ministries, praise danced, and occasionally taught at the Bible College.

I was taking my son back to school, a four-hour drive each way. During this trip, my pastor offered to take the ride with me. He wanted to pray in my son's room and check out the campus. After all, he was like family. He was my spiritual father.

All went well on the ride there. Then "it" happened. He began to tell me how unhappy he was in his marriage. He began to tell me how wicked his mother-in-law was and how he was going to get him a girlfriend. The things that he said about his wife broke my heart. I couldn't believe he was saying this about my mother in the ministry. He was painting her as a monster, and I knew better. He reached out his hand and touched my hair as it rested on my shoulder. My response to him was, "The devil is a liar." He withdrew and we continued the ride as though nothing happened, but I knew that things were about to change.

As time went by and he learned of my dating, he became really overbearing. I decided to visit my "friend" during a visit home. When he heard that I was going home and that my "friend" lived in New Orleans he said, "Well you ain't moving back and I hope he knows that."

During this trip, he called me, and I just allowed the phone to ring. I was amazed at his trickery because I knew it was him calling from his wife's phone, as she later revealed to me. Once I got home, he called me and asked if my "friend kissed me or tried to get out of the way with me." I was livid. Although fuming with indignation, I answered. I respected him as my father in the ministry, but this was starting to feel really WRONG.

After several instances like that, I called his wife and disclosed to her his overbearing attitude toward me which was making me uncomfortable. She lovingly advised me to set my boundaries, disclosing only ministry information and nothing else. She went on to express that he truly cared about me and wanted the best for me, but she didn't know the whole story. I hadn't told her yet about the car ride.

As the months passed, he didn't relent. He continued to make snide remarks, which showcased his possessiveness towards me. He was beginning to change and be overtaken by that very character weakness that he often preached about and now succumb to. I began to feel like that little girl again and was afraid. This church was my family and had been there before my real family relocated to Houston. The separation anxiety was intense as I couldn't believe this was happening again.

I knew it was over one day, when I was dressed in my clergy attire, heading out to minister. We were scheduled to minister at the prison this Saturday in particular. As I walked out of the door to leave, I turned around and ran to my bedroom, closed the door, and began to weep. I didn't know what to do with my ball of emotions. I finally had enough! I needed to worship and serve in peace. So, I told my family what transpired, and then I scheduled a meeting with the pastor's wife. Some may say that I had no place to do such a thing and that's okay but it's what I needed to do. We spoke, I tendered my letter of resignation and moved on. I was not going to be that intimidated little girl who would shrink back allowing herself to be revictimized anymore. I took authority in the mighty name of Jesus and shut that wicked spirit down!

It has been twelve years since all of that happened and it has really been hard recovering. How do you serve for five years, love your worship experience, and then have it turn out like that? The most difficult part is that my mother truly loved him as her pastor. When we left that church, she never joined another one. Her heart was still there. I guess it's ironic, but I can understand.

I don't believe in coincidences. Somehow, he accidentally called my sister and learned that my mother was critically ill so he went to visit her. When we arrived for a visit, the nurses kept telling us how my mother was so excited because "her pastor" came to see her. I smiled because I was happy for her, being that she was in her last days.

Today, I am still close with his now ex-wife and I love her larger than life. I spent many nights praying that he would find someone like her, as she was a blessing to him and me! She is by far one of the most anointed women I have ever been blessed to meet and I thank God for her. She will always be my spiritual mother and lifesaver, literally. I continue to pray for her and recently flew to Atlanta to spend time with her. My plan going forward is to visit every March, as well as attend her woman's conference. To date, I continue to pray for him, as I know he relocated and started another ministry. I pray for his total deliverance and that he walks in obedience to God's Word and pastors in a way that is pleasing to God.

Unfortunately, my spiritual warfare in the church was not over. Yes, it gets worse. Just when I thought all was well, Satan unleashed another blow. *James 1:2-3 says, "Count it all joy when you fall into various trials, knowing that the testing of your faith produces* patience." Actually, I must admit that this perpetual warfare was so taxing that as David wrote, "I would have lost heart, *unless I had believed That I would see the goodness of the Lord in the land of the living. Wait on the Lord; Be of good courage, and He shall strengthen your heart; Wait, I say, on the Lord! Psalm 27:13-14*

Chapter 25: Lifeline

After all that I encountered in the church, this would take me to the brink of death. Bayou St. John was one of my favorite spots. I often walked my niece's dog by this body of water. Typically, it was a place where I've gone to clear my head, but on this day, I wanted to drive my car into it and end it. The pills hadn't worked as the pain in my body was excruciating. On a deeper level, the emotional pain of another failed marriage overlaid in rejection, compounded with feelings of not being good enough all came flooding back to me like the roaring waves of the muddy Mississippi. And as if that was not enough, then came the intrusion of embarrassment. How do I face those that "told me so?" Those thoughts had me feeling like everyone would see the self-imposed scarlet letter of shame.

All of this confusion was going through my head so much so that I could not even hear God anymore. So, I started to doubt Him. I thought, "Was He even there? Who would understand? What was my purpose anymore? Why do I keep going back to the church? Was I called? Does it work?" I definitely had more questions than answers at this point, but the Earth stood silent and still. It was as if I was Adam in the Garden of Eden and was all alone. Then I got that call from my spiritual mother that diffused my torment. She told me that she believed me. She believed everything I told her about the pastor and her now former husband. She went on to say that out of all the women in the church, she knew my integrity and that she would always be there for me. She has kept that promise to this day.

Chapter 26: The Deadly Dating Game!

Early June 2013, once more, I decided to try my hand at dating. I threw my hat in the mix and decided to try a Christian dating site. I figured that if they took the time to go on a Christian site, they would probably be credible. Here's a taste of what I posted, "I am a warm fun-loving Southern Belle. I enjoy spending quiet time at home and watching a good movie. I enjoy nice dinners out by the river. I love my church home where I am active. I am really looking for a friendship first. If anything flourishes from that, Praise God. I think that I make a great partner because I am really at a good place in life. I have peace and don't really care to play games. I know what's important and I've learned to cherish the little things in life. When first getting to know me, I might come across as very serious however, once you get to know me, you'll find that I am quite the practical joker. I love a good laugh! NOTE: If you are Legally Separated, I will NOT respond to you on ANY LEVEL BECAUSE YOU ARE STILL MARRIED!! Clear up that relationship. Once again, why am

I addressing this? I have had married men pose as divorced or single only to find that they are still very married. Too old for games."

Yes, this was my actual post. I connected with someone that really appeared to be nice and we decided to take our profiles down and become exclusive. Our relationship progressed quickly. I believe I let my guards down quickly because, yes, he was a pastor in Alabama and I desperately wanted to believe he was living for Christ. My profile was very clear and to the point. We discussed what we both wanted and he agreed to abstinence, etc.

At the time, I was busy with my job directing a pre-collegiate program at a local college in New Orleans. Due to my job responsibilities, I really couldn't travel, so he would come to visit me. I was okay with that. In retrospect, I can say that I didn't do my due diligence because I was too busy "doing life." My family had concerns because we were moving too fast. It's not that they had anything against him, but it wasn't like me to throw caution to the wind.

Dr. Kimberlyn Negret

The date was set 12/31/13. After my family had so many reservations, we eloped 12/30/13 with my wedding dress in the closet, wedding venue unused, and caterer paid for. I guess you get the picture. Again, in retrospect, this worked out for him because on 12/30/13, he stated that he was thinking about postponing the wedding. I told him that if he wanted to do that, it was okay, but after all that I had been through with my family, we, he and I, would have to part ways. We both dressed, proceeded to the courthouse, and were married. No walking down the aisle. No candlelight ceremony. No reception. What a drastic difference from what was planned. I talked myself into it being okay, because after all, it was for love.

We were delaying our honeymoon because everyone knows that New Year's Eve service is important. I thought I'd be able to enjoy service in Alabama. That didn't happen. He went to his service, and I got to stay at the hotel we had selected as our "honeymoon" destination. I was just married, yet alone. It went down quickly shortly thereafter. We were planning to plant another church in Birmingham once I left my job in June 2014.

I was told that prior to us marrying, he and his ex-wife pastored a church and after they divorced, she would make appearances from time to time. Because I am always on a quest to preserve peace, I thought it best to confront her or let her have the church. I was not going to disrupt the service on that day. My basis was *"God is not the author of confusion." (1 Corinthians 14:33.)* He was reluctant to let the church go though, so I exercised what I thought was patience.

January 2014, while he was visiting me, I received a message through Facebook. It was a wedding picture of him and his "ex" wife. I confronted him about receiving it and he simply explained it away as, "She's just jealous that we are together." It made sense to me, so I let it go. Then I confided in my daughter. She then spoke with the woman and was told that they were still very much married. Her exact words were, "If we're divorced, I don't know anything about it." I thought to myself, "What a fool! You should know if your still married or if you're divorced."

March 30th was his birthday. He was supposed to come and visit after his church service, but I didn't hear from him. Now my suspicion was heightened. I spoke with my spiritual mother/mentor, and she guided me through the process. I went the entire next week as though nothing was wrong. We talked several times a day, like always. He never knew what was to come. I worked the morning and spoke with him as I was picking up my daughter's SUV. April 5, 2014, I made my way to Akron, AL. During the ride, I prayed and prayed and prayed. My mentor had me prepare a list. It went something like this: If I see him with another woman I will do (blank). If I see his car at their previous home, I will … If I catch him at church with her I will… After going through this list over and over in my head, I was programmed because after all, I was in Akron, AL all by myself.

As I was driving, he called and I prayed that the GPS wouldn't go off to let him know that I was there. I was on my way to the house. Something inside me told me not to and to just go to the hotel and guess what? The phone rings. It was him! He told me that the police had just left the house. They were looking for his son who was implicated in a home burglary. I proceeded to get something to eat so that I could hunker down until the morning. He spared me again.

April 6, 2014, I woke up to the rain hitting the window of the hotel. I got dressed and headed out. I wasn't sure when Sunday school started, so I wanted to get there early. I ventured out and my stomach was turning. After waiting about an hour, I saw the car pull up. It was him. He was not alone. The passenger side door opened, and a woman emerged. Then the two back doors opened, and it was his son and another young man. At that time, I had my foot on the brake and thought to myself, should I just mow him down right here? He flew out of the car and ran into the church before I could do anything. After sitting there a few minutes, a woman came to the window of my car. She inquired as to how she could help me. I then told her "My name is Dr. Kimberlyn Negret-Nickson, I am

Pastor Nickson's wife." She looked confused. I then presented her with a packet I had prepared in case anyone at the church gave me any trouble. She looked at the packet that contained pictures taken at the courthouse, pictures of our rings, marriage license, etc. She then announced that she was his wife too. At that point, she asked if I wanted to go into the church to talk. I said no. I didn't want to get out of the car and be vulnerable. So, she went into the church to get him. He was gone. He ran out of the back door of the church. His wife and I talked for a few more minutes and I left. I was on my way back home. I saw what I needed to see. A few minutes later, my phone rings and it was him. He wanted to know what was in the packet. I told him had he not run and stayed to face the music like a man, he would know.

It was a long ride home. At one point, I was totally lost as it stormed and I lost my bearings. I prayed and prayed that I could get back to the interstate safely. I was so afraid that he would catch up to me and run me off the road. The gravity of what just transpired just got real. I had to come to terms that I was married to a bigamist. Then "it" hit me. I purposed to save myself for my husband and got conned. No amount of money could give me back what he violated and stole from me. Now, I was mad!

The next week I scheduled an appointment with an attorney. After telling him my most embarrassing story, he promised he would handle the annulment and then we could proceed to a criminal case. I thought it would be an easy case as I later learned that my attorney was an assistant District Attorney in New Orleans and an ad hoc traffic judge. I paid him the retainer, plus the first installment. After a few months of not hearing anything, I contacted him to check the status of the case and he told me I needed to pay the rest of the bill. I felt as though I was getting the run around and needed to take another route.

I had only disclosed this to my daughter, son, and two close friends. One of my friends advised me and said it was time to go to the police, so I did. At this time, I was so fragile, taking pills to sleep, pills for migraines, pills for my stomach... Pills, pills, pills. I found myself at the 4th district police department about to tell my embarrassing story to them. I got to the front desk and asked if I could speak with someone in private. The officer on desk duty asked why? I went on to tell her it was a very private matter. They were so kind, they allowed me to be interviewed in the hallway at a desk. So much for privacy.

After a few weeks passed by, I went to get my copy of the police report. It was wrong and I was livid. At that point, I went to the Internal Affairs office, as directed by the staff, where I got my police report. Well, I got as far as the front door when I was told by one of their officers to go back to the 4th district and speak with the supervisors there. So, I headed back to the 4th district. Once there, I met with the acting commander. He listened to my story and then he called in another officer. Wouldn't you know it, it was the same officer that was rude to me on the first occasion. I was in tears and emptied the contents of my purse on their desk. I said, "This may not be a murder case, but my life is turned upside down now and these are the medications I'm taking just to make it through the day. I just need you to do your job." I also reported the attorney as he had essentially stolen my money and not done anything regarding my case.

The police told me that a warrant for his arrest would be made. Shortly thereafter, he was arrested. It was a Saturday morning, and I was sitting at my desk at work when the phone rang. It was none other than his wife. She said, "He told me to call you". I said, "OKAY and ...." She went on to say that he had been arrested and I told her that I had nothing else to discuss with her. He was rightfully arrested, and I was done talking. I then called the police department in Alabama and was advised that after two weeks, if the New Orleans Police Department hadn't extradited him, he would be released. I called a few times per week to see if he was released because I knew him, and he was going to be angry. He was picked up around Thanksgiving and was going to miss the holiday with his "family." The police advised me that he waived extradition and was waiting to be transported to New Orleans. That never happened. The New Orleans Police Department never went to get him, and he was released. I was devastated, scared, and felt as though I needed to watch my back. After all of this, I came to the realization that I didn't know this man or what he was capable of. None the less, I wanted justice, and it alluded me.

One of my friends saw that I was distraught, tired, and weary. I phoned the office of the Attorney General in Baton Rouge and told them the entire story. I started receiving calls from the DA's office and police department. They were back on the case and my former attorney contacted me in regard to returning the payment. As of 2023, it still hasn't come. Reliving this nightmare all over again, I answered questions about the case. Then "it" happened again. He was arrested and sat in jail for weeks. Wouldn't you know it, he was released again because the NOPD didn't go to pick him up again!

My annulment was already done, and I was legally free from him. Then, I learned he had married again. As stated before, my name means "seeker of truth", and I couldn't let this situation go. Periodically, I'd search his name to see if he were up to his old ways. Something inside of me kept telling me that he was still up to his shenanigans. His being married again was interesting because he was still married to the first wife. I was unsettled at finding this out and certainly didn't want the new wife to hurt as badly as I had been, so I attempted to find her, to no avail. The clock kept ticking and finally the first wife divorced him. She took possession of their church, and he was left with nothing. Hmmmmm… nothing but the deception that he held so dearly to his heart.

He was now on to another wife. December 2015, he married again. His collateral damage now spanned from Alabama to Louisiana and Georgia. Now, I'm furious! The state of Louisiana and the city of New Orleans didn't take this situation seriously. The former Governor Bobby Jindal didn't do much for our state, but he did revise a racketeering law which states, "A bill broadening Louisiana's racketeering laws to include a range of crimes including human trafficking, kidnapping, bigamy, and the sale of children has been signed into law. Gov. Bobby Jindal signed House Bill 279 by Rep.

Cameron Henry, R-Metairie. Racketeering laws are utilized by prosecutors to target members of an organization engaged in criminal activities and the measure would allow tougher penalties against groups engaged in those crimes.

The bill adds the following crimes to the definition of racketeering statute: female genital mutilation, aggravated kidnapping of a child younger than 13, human trafficking, trafficking of children for sexual purposes, bigamy, abetting in bigamy, and the sale of minor children.

Anyone or a group of people found to be repeatedly committing any of those crimes on an organized basis would be charged with racketeering, which is an automatic felony offense and punishable with a fine of $1 million, imprisonment for not more than 50 years, or both." Supporters state, "it's chiefly aimed at groups of human traffickers, illegal adoption rings and bigamist colonies."
(http://www.nola.com/politics/index.ssf/2013/06/jindal_signs_bill_adding_human.html).

The state of Alabama captured him twice only to be forced to let him go because the New Orleans Police Department didn't handle their responsibility. Because he has yet to be held accountable for his actions, an innocent baby was brought into this mess of a situation. May 2015, I located a baby registry for his third wife. Yes, they were expecting a baby. I didn't know the exact date, but I knew it was coming.

December 2015, he married again. As soon as I saw the post, I struggled if I should message her. It took me a month to finally get the nerve to contact her. On 2/8/15, I messaged the woman in Atlanta, GA. The very brief conversation went like this. "I struggled if I should send a message to you. I am not certain if Jimmie ever told you about me, but I married him 12/30/13. In January 2015, our marriage was annulled under the grounds of bigamy. He promised to pay legal fees, that hasn't happened. The district attorney is still seeking to press charges. What hurts the most is that he took something special from me and I can't get that back, all while knowing he was married. He went as far as meeting with my pastor, etc. I pray you did your homework. My intent is NOT to hurt you, but I refuse to allow him to treat women like he has. (*1 Timothy 3:2*) Several days later, I received her reply, "I thank you for sending this message. I have felt that. The Lord also told me he was still married. I just haven't said anything yet. God bless you for stepping up. The day we got married the Lord said He was still married."

There is a very staunch difference between the two of us. She decided to stay in it. In October 2015, she wrote a post, and it went like this: "My Transparency!! I married a spirit that used a Godly man to destroy all that I had. The marriage wasn't legal, but the trespass was lethal, because other souls were attached. That spirit left behind a seed, and in this season, births reason for me to take my life back, and I glorify the Lord God for that." I thought to myself, she finally got the truth. A few years later, she announced that she had cancer and ultimately succumbed to it. Needless to say, he was nowhere to be found.

I'll be transparent for a minute. I wanted him to hurt. He has yet to apologize, manufactured damage and moved on. That is his MO. He truly doesn't care about anyone except himself. Months before catching him in Alabama with his first wife, there were occasions that I thought something was not right. When I approached him, he said that "I was being evil, and I needed to pray to see the good in people." For a while I took that bait and believed that I was thinking negative. Believing and hoping he was right, could not override God's still small voice. If I was right, I was made a fool of.

This book has a theme of forgiveness which is more for us than the perpetrator. I came to terms with the fact that harboring anger was like drinking poison and expecting him to die. If I waited for an apology, I was only stagnating myself in a state of misery. Knowing that he was lying and leaving collateral damage everywhere he went, I tried to find a balance between peace and anger. I've struggled with if I should continue to write the book or let the dust settle between the pages and walk away, but something continued to compel me.

I believe that the state of the church today is at best, in ruins. False prophets have placed themselves behind the pulpit and have misconstrued the Word of God. They are "spiritual pimps" who have pilfered their disenfranchised congregations and have slept with and raped their children and women. What respect is found in this? Why do we continue to allow it to happen? Have we replaced God with them? Who are we really worshipping?

I was going to church to find God, but because of my hurt as a child, I was looking for approval from God through men. Men that were just as broken, if not more broken than I was. This is not what God called His people to do or be. On the contrary, this is when man calls himself. As written in *Jeremiah 23*, false prophets, prophesying, in the name of The Lord, yet He has not sent them. This is a blatant act of Preying while Praying. To repent is to turn away and not do it again. As far as I know, he's had four marriages, but that's as far as I know. For a while, I thought to myself, "Why are You doing this to me, God? Why have You allowed something that You knew was so precious to me to be taken, again. Why are You allowing him to continue this path of destruction with all of this collateral damage to follow? Why?"

I was left with only an opportunity to take hold of and reclaim my dignity, fortified with a voice to speak my truth "for such a time as this". He's been given ample opportunities to change his ways in private but refused. Now what was done in the dark will be revealed. How can he preach on purity when he is perverse? How can he preach on the sanctity of marriage when he is an adulterer and a bigamist? How can he lead a home when he destroys homes? How can he speak on truth when he is actively living a lie?

This incident left me feeling very empty, used, devalued, and hurt. It took me years to pick myself up and put the pieces back together. I trusted him with my deepest hurts, and he didn't care. His only concern was to have his way without any repercussions. So far, his actions garnered impunity. Some might think, I wasn't married that long, so, why does it hurt? To them I say again, he took away my choice to make an informed decision as well as my desire to remain celibate until I was married. He went in knowing full well that he was married, as well as God's Law with the biblical rules of engagement about *"Let every man have his own wife and every women have her own husband."* *(1Corinthians 7:2)* He chose to ignore and distort them to suit his own appetite. I have no hatred, but there is a strong disdain for those who *"Profess Christ with their mouths but their hearts are far from Him.* *(Matthew 15:8-9)* My goal was to stop a 5th wife from feeling his wrath of destruction. So, for such a time as this, I will expose the lie that almost took me out. Am I still actively seeking "justice?" The answer is no. I've left retribution up to God. He handles all things well. I also know that there will be those that say I should have let it go long ago. I truly understand and respect your opinion, but today the abuse stops. I have set my own boundaries aiming to live life to the fullest and have peace at all costs. I am no longer seeking punishment. I seek justice through Him.

In case you're wondering, yes, I have forgiven him too. As for me, have I truly gotten "it", in reference to "understanding the trauma that produced this cycle of disastrous relationships?" The answer is, yes, on some levels while others are still evolving and maturing.

As far as my long-lost friend Jacob is concerned, the truth is, while going through all of this, I was simply too embarrassed to even reach out to him. He was busy with life, his church/ministry, his wife, and kids. But as some would say, as the universe would have it, in 2018 we reconnected. I was transparent about everything, and he simply listened. There was no condemnation and to date he has never brought it up. We are still exceptionally good friends. We go to brunch from time to time and he attends my grandkids/his God children's events. We are in a good place. I guess that could be expected after twenty plus years of friendship that survived and stood the test of trials. We have had our highs and Lord knows we have had our lows, but through it all, we are now intentional about maintaining and nurturing our friendship. My prayer has always been for him to be happy and fulfilled and it has not changed.

There are some very valuable lessons that I have learned throughout the course of this journey:

1. Although "it" gets hard sometimes, *I am anointed for these trials and must "endure hardship as a good soldier." (2 Timothy 2:3)* I remember the first time I heard, *"I know that you get tired sometimes, that you feel overwhelmed sometimes, but you were anointed for this.* So, I must press on.

"Not that I have already attained, or am already perfected; but I press on, that I may lay hold of that for which Christ Jesus has also laid hold of me. Brethren, I do not count myself to have apprehended; but one thing I do, forgetting those things which are behind and reaching forward to those things which are ahead, I press toward the goal for the prize of the upward call of God in Christ Jesus." Philippians 3:12-14

My spiritual mother prophesied to me that there was purpose in my pain. I was anointed to manage this load and once I learned to carry the weight, I would be able to help others. I now mentor a few young ladies and I am amazed at how my journey of pain to purpose has evolved.

2. Although men and women break promises, God is a God who will never leave you nor forsake you. *"Let your conduct be without covetousness; be content with such things as you have. For He Himself has said, "I will never leave you nor forsake you." Hebrews 13:5.* He will never break a promise. I now know that God is a God that provides. He is Jehovah Jireh.

3. During all my trials, I must, "consider it all joy." *"My brethren, count it all joy when you fall into various trials, knowing that the testing of your faith produces patience. But let patience have its perfect work, that you may be perfect and complete, lacking nothing." James 1:2-4*

4. I must see myself as God sees me and believe that I am fearfully and wonderfully made. *"I will praise You, for I am fearfully and wonderfully made; Marvelous are Your works, and that my soul knows very well." Psalm 139:14*

5. Although I am hard pressed on every side, God is with me. *"We are hard pressed on every side, yet not crushed; we are perplexed, but not in despair; persecuted, but not forsaken; struck down, but not destroyed" 2 Corinthians 4:8-9*

6. Although I have made mistakes, God has totally forgiven me for there is no condemnation in Christ Jesus. *"There is therefore now no condemnation to those who are in Christ Jesus, who do not walk according to the flesh, but according to the Spirit." Romans 8:1*

7. God has a purpose and destiny for my life. *"For I know the thoughts that I think toward you, says the Lord, thoughts of peace and not of evil, to give you a future and a hope." Jeremiah 29:11*

8. God has given me a vision and I must run with it. *"Then the Lord answered me and said: "Write the vision and make it*

plain on tablets, that he may run who reads it. For the vision is yet for an appointed time; but at the end it will speak, and it will not lie. Though it tarries, wait for it; because it will surely come, it will not tarry." Habakkuk 2:2-3

9. What my purpose is. *"The spirit of the Lord God is upon me, Because the Lord has anointed me to bring the good news to the afflicted; He has sent me to bind up the brokenhearted, to proclaim liberty to the captives and freedom to prisoners; 2 - To proclaim the favorable year of the Lord and the day of vengeance of our God; To comfort all who mourn."* Isaiah 61:1-2

10. His grace is sufficient. *"And He said to me, My grace is sufficient for you, for My strength is made perfect in weakness."* Therefore, most gladly I will rather boast in my infirmities, that the power of Christ may rest upon me." 2 Corinthians 12:9

11. Although I am single, I am not alone. *"Yea, though I walk through the valley of the shadow of death, I will fear no evil:*

for thou art with me; thy rod and thy staff they comfort me." Psalm 23:4

12. If I had not gone through all of this, I would not have been prepared to accept my call into the ministry. There is a passage of scripture that I use to encourage myself when I am feeling somewhat discouraged. That passage is: *"If you have run with footmen and they have tired you out, Then how can you compete with horses? If you fall down in a land of peace; how will you do in the thicket of the Jordan?"* Jeremiah 12: 5

13. To hold my head up and look forward to where God sends, for what the rest of my journey will unfold. *"For I know the plans that I have for you, declares the Lord, plans for welfare and not for calamity to give you a future and a hope."* Jeremiah 29:11

14. How to run this race. *"Therefore, I run thus: not with uncertainty. Thus, I fight not as one who beats the air. But I discipline my body and bring it into subjection, lest, when I have preached to others, I should become disqualified."* 1 Corinthians 9:26-27

My prayer is that my journey ends where the streets are paved with gold. So, I encourage you my brethren to *"Watch yourselves that you do not lose what we have accomplished, but that you may receive a full reward."* 2 John 1:8

"And twelve gates were pearls; each one of the gates was a single pearl. And the street of the city was pure gold, like transparent glass." Revelations 21:21.

See you on the other side of pain and into the light of abundant life!

The Journey continues.

The End

Dr. Kimberlyn Negret

About the Author

Born and raised in New Orleans and a product of the New Orleans Public School System, Kimberlyn Negret, Ph.D., beat the odds! Breaking generational cycles of abuse and poverty, she attended Southern University, New Orleans, LA where she earned a Bachelor of Science degree in Criminal Justice, a Master's Degree in Psychology from Our Lady of the Lake University, San Antonio, TX and Master's Degree in Christian Counseling and her Ph.D. in Theology from Cornerstone University, Lake Charles, LA. . Her educational journey was the genesis of her beginning towards healing and wholeness.

In 2002, Kimberlyn became an ordained minister and ultimately ordained as an elder and assistant pastor where she has presided over children's, liturgical dance, and women's ministries. Currently an educator in the Houston, TX area, Kimberlyn has spent the past twenty plus years educating students with special needs along with first generation college students. She is also an experienced Mental Health Practitioner who is a childhood survivor of sexual abuse and domestic violence. The trauma experienced during the course of her journey called "life," has fueled her passion to work with those deemed underserved or at risk. The keys to her success in these areas are attributed to her facing the ACE's (Adverse Childhood Experiences) in her past and coming to terms with the trauma. God has equipped her with the tenacity to fight the good fight of faith and to empower those she comes in contact with to also fight for their healing and deliverance. Her desire is not to leave any sister behind as they journey towards healing, wholeness and deliverance.

Dr. Kimberlyn Negret

A portion of the proceeds from Fresh Spirit Publishing goes towards Fresh Spirit Wellness for Women, a non-profit organization, 5Ol(c), founded in 1997. FSWW assist men, women and youth who have been verbally, emotionally, physically or sexually abused by providing counseling, case management, and court advocacy, workshops, and seminars to those in search of healing and support.

www.freshspirit.org

Made in the USA
Coppell, TX
28 September 2024

37836674R00114